WHITE COMPOSITIONS
1995 - 2024

ANTHONY AMES
ARCHITECT

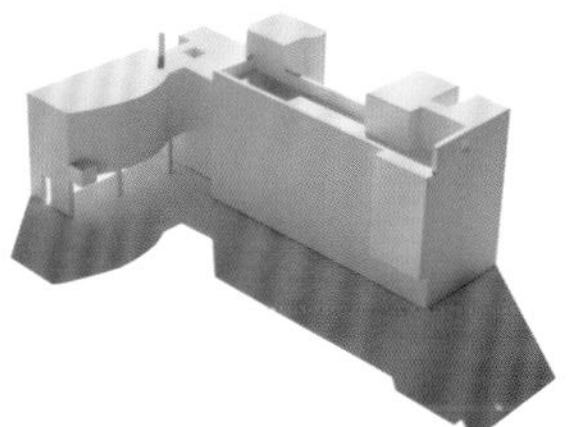

Preceding page: Le Corbusier, *Villa La Roche Jeanneret*, Acrylic on Wood, model, 2024.

WHITE COMPOSITIONS
1995 - 2024

ANTHONY AMES
ARCHITECT

INTRODUCTION
BY
CLARA SYME

ESSAYS
BY
ALAN BALFOUR
COURTNEY COFFMAN
PETER EISENMAN

POSTSCRIPT
BY
DAISY AMES

ORO EDITIONS

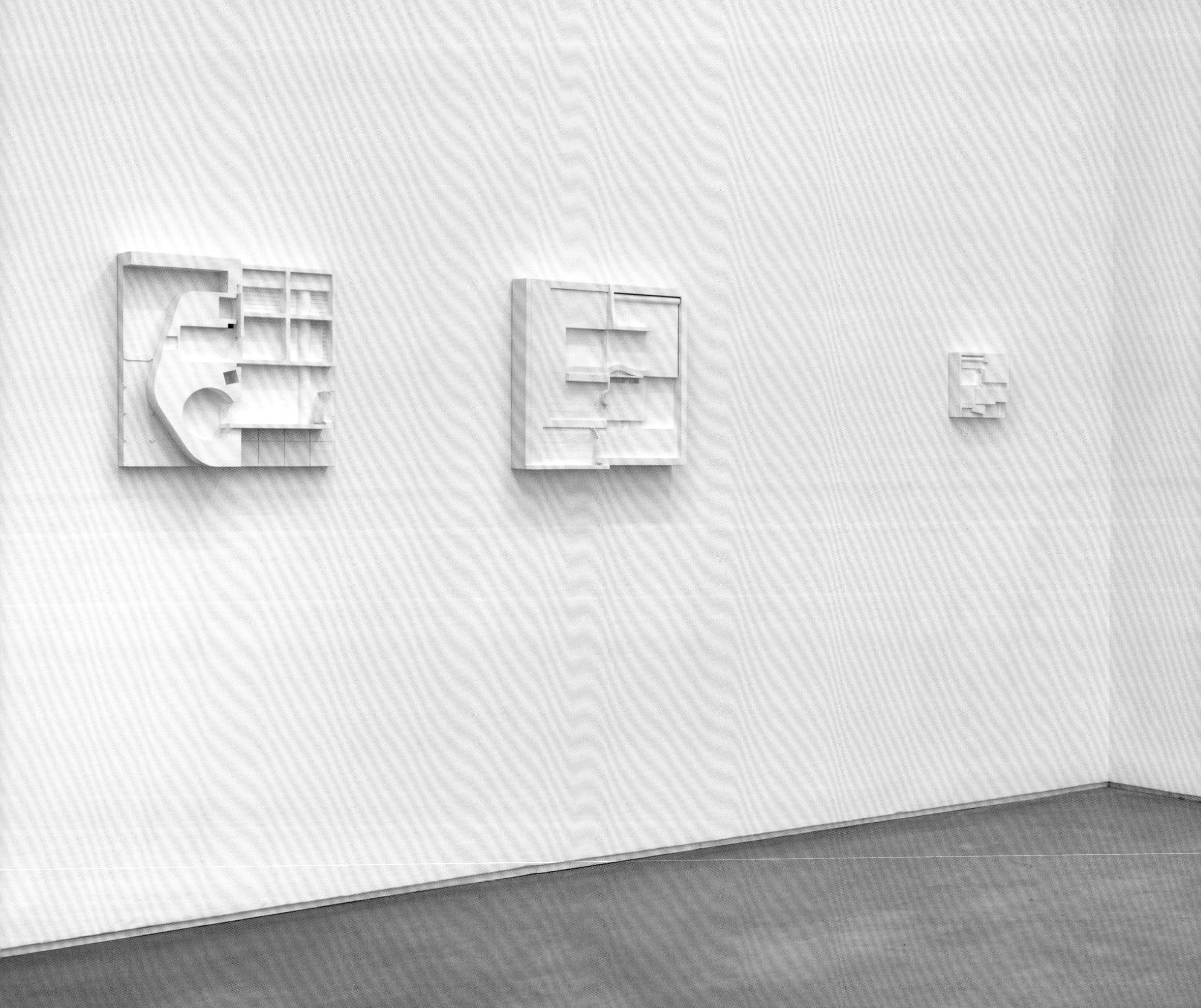

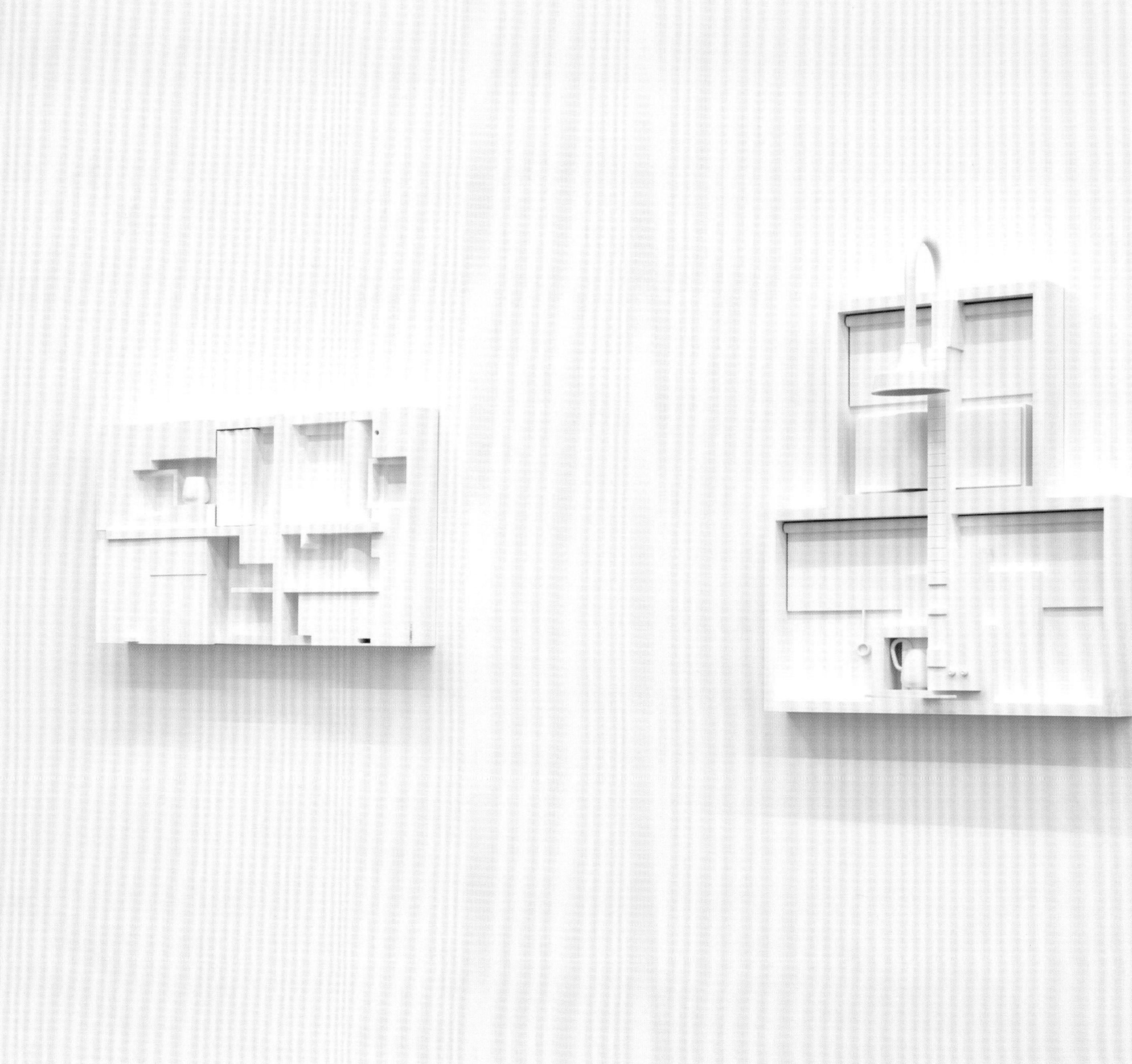

ORO Editions
Publishers of Architecture, Art, and Design
Gordon Goff: Publisher

www.oroeditions.com
info@oroeditions.com

Published by ORO Editions

Author: AAA
Designer: AAA
Project Manager: Jake Anderson

10 9 8 7 6 5 4 3 2 1 First Edition

ISBN: 978-1-966515-17-3

Prepress and Print work by ORO Editions Inc.
Printed in China

ORO Editions makes a continuous effort to minimize the overall carbon footprint of its publications. As part of this goal, ORO, in association with Global ReLeaf, arranges to plant trees to replace those used in the manufacturing of the paper produced for its books. Global ReLeaf is an international campaign run by American Forests, one of the world's oldest nonprofit conservation organizations. Global ReLeaf is American Forests' education and action program that helps individuals, organizations, agencies, and corporations improve the local and global environment by planting and caring for trees.

Preceding page: *White Compositions* exhibition at a83 Gallery, New York, New York, 2024.
See also pp. 12, 16, 22 and 26.

In 1923 Mallet-Stevens told me: “We ought to patent our ideas or at least protect them with trademarks.”

Certainly not! It is the nature of ideas to belong to everybody. There are two choices: to give ideas or to take ideas. We do both, really; we gladly give out our ideas; in return we use, we exploit for our own purposes, ideas scattered through all areas - ideas which one day, in whole or in part, end up helping us. Ideas are public property. To share one’s ideas, well, there is simply no other way!

Le Corbusier

Précisions Sur Un État Présent de l’Architecture et de l’Urbanisme. Vincent, Fréal & Cie., Paris, 1960.

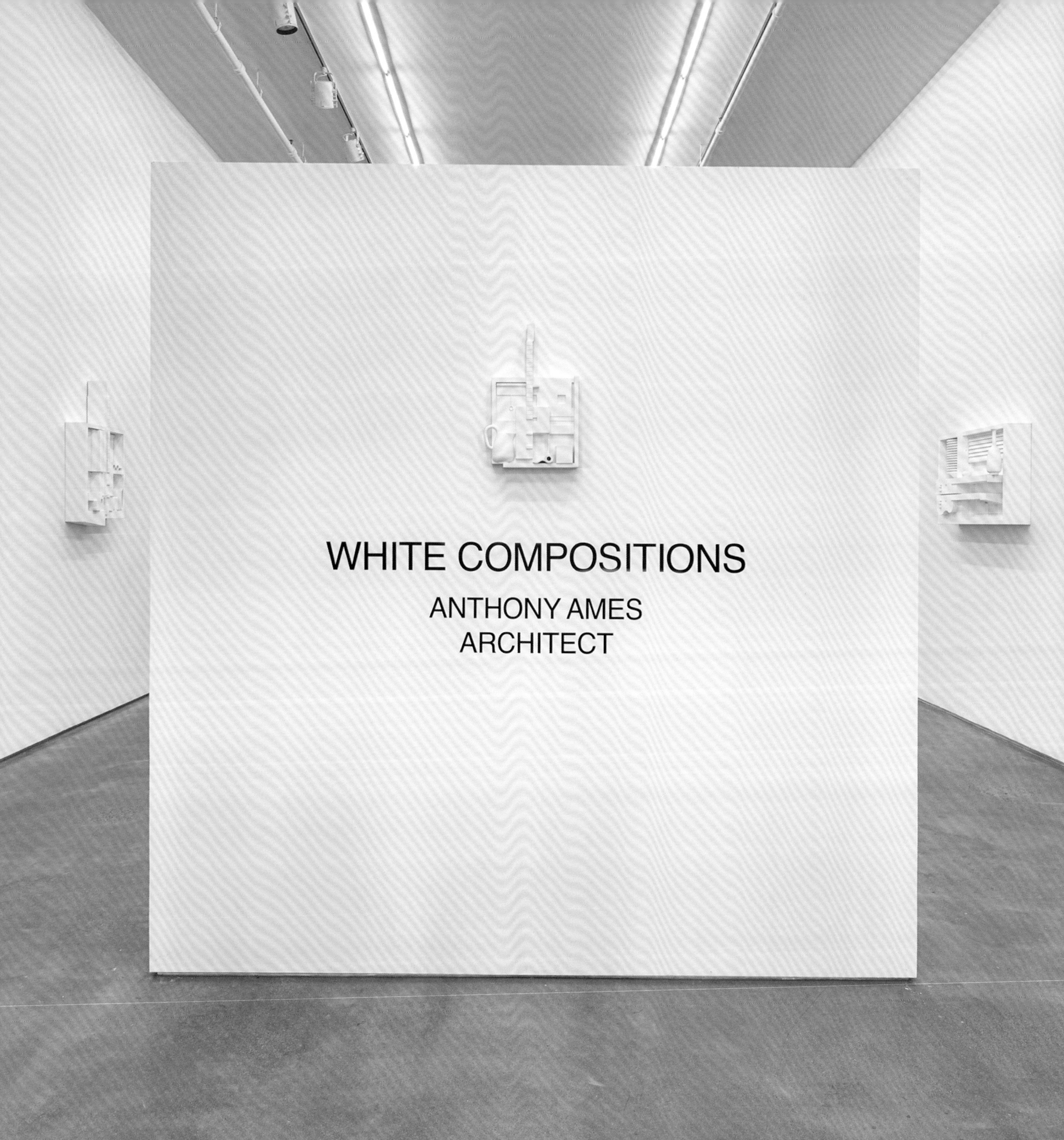
WHITE COMPOSITIONS
ANTHONY AMES
ARCHITECT

CONTENTS

INTRODUCTION

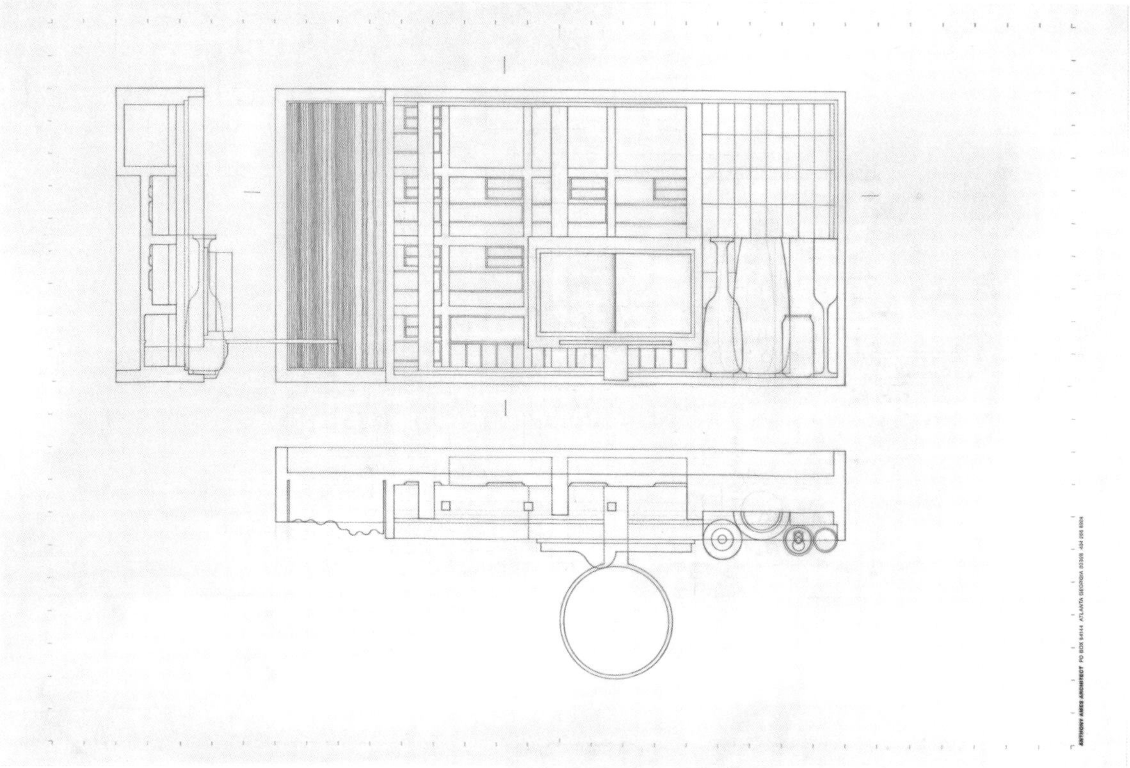

Based in Atlanta, Georgia, Anthony Ames has operated his eponymous architecture office since 1976 and began painting in 1984. Ames' *White Compositions*—a series of 11 monochromatic relief wall sculptures—originate from and elaborate on the architect's painting practice, closely attending to proportion, layout, recurring forms, and motifs found within both his artistic and built works. His paintings—as described by Courtney Coffman in her previous review of Ames' solo exhibition at a83 Gallery in New York—"oscillate somewhere between the formality of a still life, the dynamism of sculptural relief, and the juxtaposed delight of collage." A natural evolution in Ames' practice, the 11 wall sculptures are accompanied by documents that provide insight into the precise and accomplished nature of Ames' design process: from buildings to art.

Despite their monochromatic simplicity, Ames' *White Compositions* provide manifold readings. Emphasized by the use of an all-white palette, the 11 pieces are highly formal, operating through the play of light and shadows on volumes and within voids. Each sculpture is also a rigorous geometric and compositional exercise in which spatial complexity is expressed within a relatively shallow depth of six inches or less. Meticulously constructed, each composition is designed by Ames through sketches and then elaborated as orthographic drawings, forming a complete set of dimensioned elevations and sections (see Appendix 2 pp. 71-78). The drawing sets—one for each composition—are masterfully drafted and supremely organized. As precursors to the relief sculptures, the drawings provide a set of instructions for construction, just as they do for his buildings. The orthographic sets expertly communicate Ames' artistic intent and his practiced manipulation of space at varying scales. The process work emphatically presents the *White Compositions* as "constructed." Preceding the execution of the physical pieces, the drawings provide insight into Ames' working method, one greatly influenced by his educational training and professional experience. His use of architectural drawing tools to execute fine art indicates a continuity in Ames' approach to his work—both as an artist and an architect.

The pieces are symbolically charged with highly specific references that speak to Ames' work and life as an architect in Georgia preoccupied with modernism, art, and basketball, among other cultural and literary meanings. Ames playfully collages architectural elements, such as facades organized by grids, with everyday (yet highly specific) objects—like a Morandi-esque vase, a Corbusian pair of glasses, a can of coke, a Gretsch guitar, or a basketball hoop. The contrast between the (supposedly) rational, objective, and universalizing characteristics of modernism in confrontation with the particular, the idiosyncratic, and the autobiographical quotidian communicates a uniquely Ames-ian sensibility that provides a distinctive and refreshing take on the 20th-century architectural movement. As thoughtfully described by Coffman, Ames' artworks "...undoubtedly communicate the 'high,' capital-A Architecture of modernism, particularly that of media- and brand-savvy figures like Corb, but they also acknowledge figures like Michael Jordan as equally influential to Ames. The latter provides a crucial catalyst for the shifting zeitgeist in architecture discourse today: uncovering alternative histories and new architectural heroes."

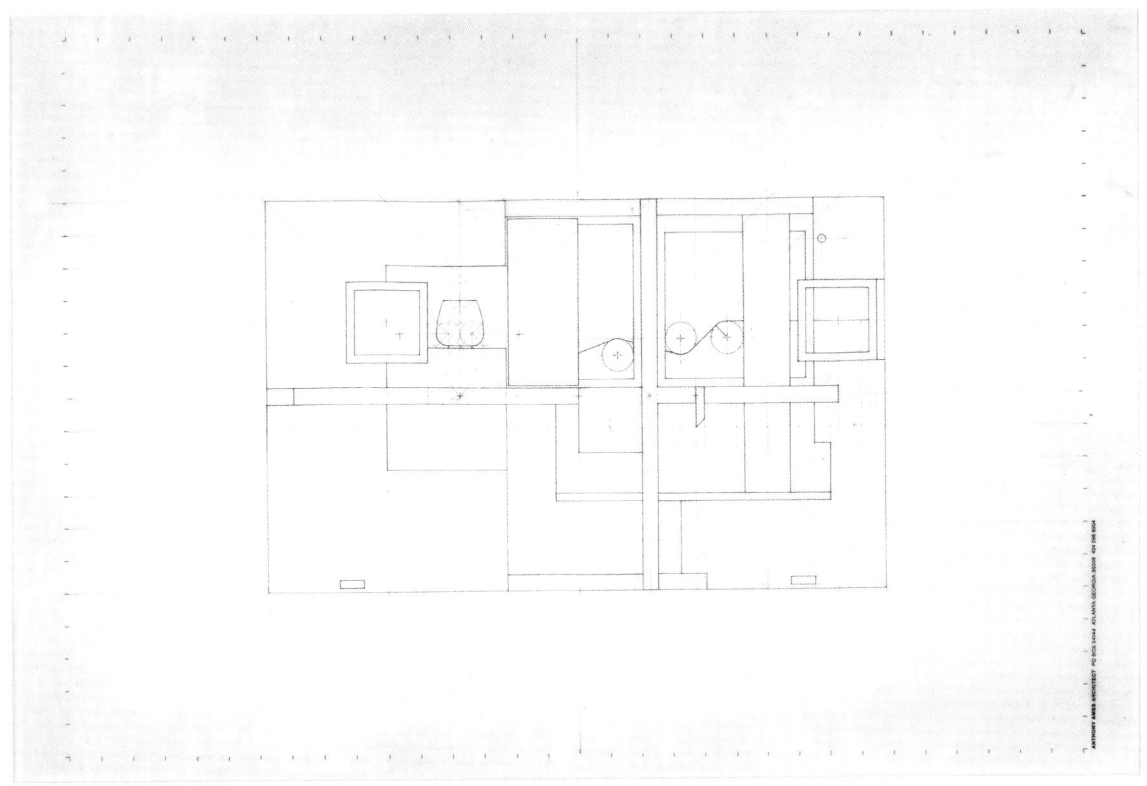

Just as Ames operates across boundaries—from architecture to art to basketball—with characteristic precision, diligence, and a sense of humor, his *White Compositions* blithely challenge the categorization of model, sculpture, painting, and drawing, fluctuating between a reading of familiarity and abstraction.

Clara Syme

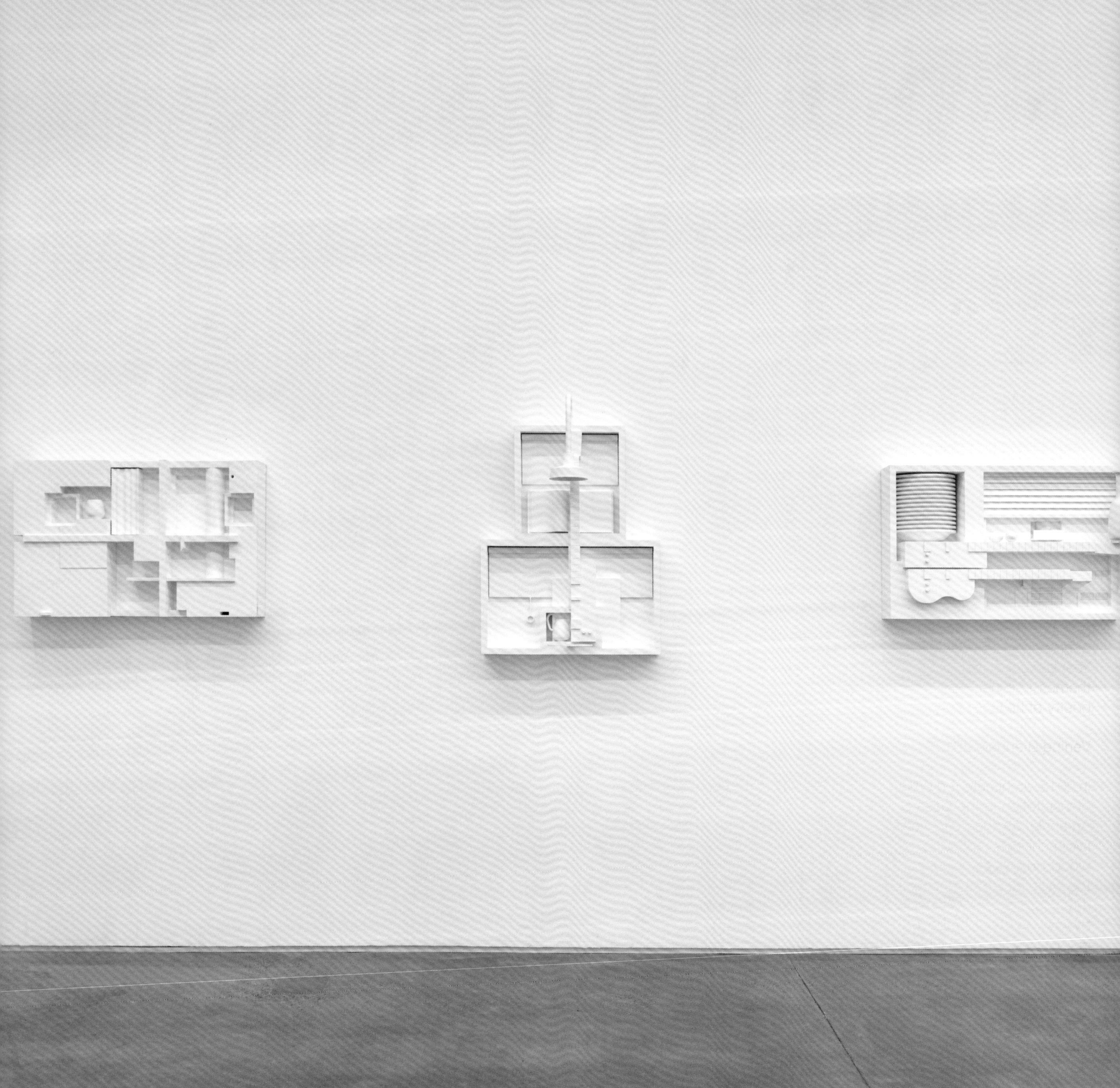

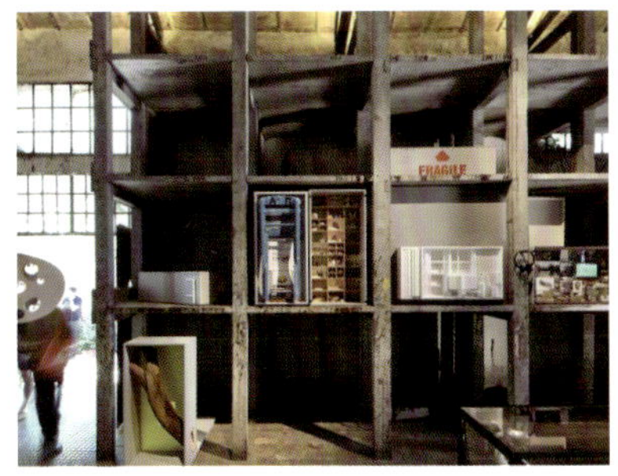

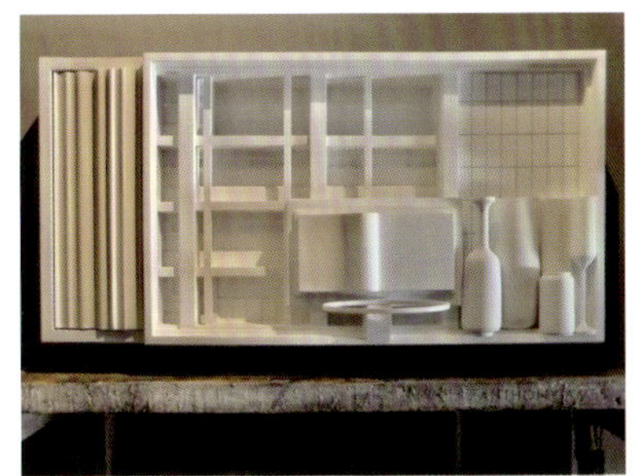

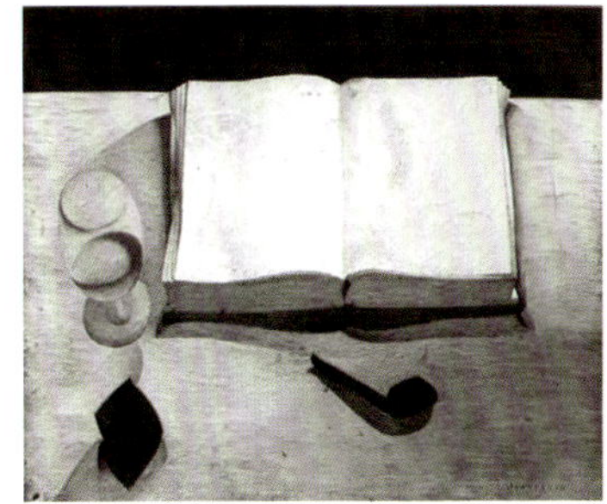

ENIGMA VARIATIONS

Approaching Anthony Ames' quiet and delicate exhibition *White Compositions* at a83 Gallery in New York, I am reminded of a well-known anecdote concerning the composer Chopin, certainly apocryphal. After he gave an exquisite performance of his *Fantasia Impromptu* and after the rapturous applause had died down, someone in the audience waved their hands and stood up, and said, "That was exhilarating Herr Chopin, but what does it mean?" In response, and with great solemnity, Chopin returned to the piano and played the work again.

Helped by Chopin I will not attempt to ascribe meaning to Ames' twelve intricate constructions. I will, however, give some background on possible sources that influenced the work and offer a personal view on the sequence of transformations that gave them form. Full disclosure: I have known the artist-architect for more than forty years and am continually impressed by his singular vision. There is no concealing what inspires him, all his creations reflect an intense pleasure in the imagination and architecture of Charles-Édouard Jeanneret, later known as Le Corbusier. Year by year and decade after decade, Ames has explored interweaving themes and harmonies that essentially reinvent and extend the visual poetry of Le Corbusier.

Venice Biennale 2012

In 2012, architects Tod Williams and Billie Tsien curated a *Wunderkammer* of inspiration in the Casa Scaffali, a small pavilion in the gardens of the Arsenale for the 2012 Venice Architecture Biennale (above left). Thirty-five architects and artists from around the world were shipped identical wood boxes and invited to fill them by creating a work that embodied the sources of their inspiration. Amidst the extraordinary variety of stuff, much of it incomprehensible, was a stark rectangular relief sculpture by Anthony Ames (above center). The composition, which reappeared in the New York exhibition, sans box, contains many of the motifs that play games in Ames' imagination: a hanging curtain, an array of vessels – vase, wine glass, and soda can – against a tiled wall, and two items which are, each in its own way, mysterious: a book and, jutting forward from the picture plane, a hoop.

In 2024, in the back room of the a83 Gallery, alongside concept sketches and construction drawings (possibly ignored by many), was the most recent composition, *White Composition 12* (page 58). It is possibly a key to much of the earlier work. On the right side of a simple shelf are an open book, a slender wine glass, and a pair of eyeglasses with a heavy circular frame that are associated with Le Corbusier. At the far left end of the shelf is a small model of a building, which after some effort I identified as the Villa La Roche Jeanneret (home of the Le Corbusier Foundation). This led me to assume that elements of Le Corbusier's architecture are probably present in many of Ames' compositions. But then, projecting from the wall high above the center of the shelf is a miniature basketball hoop, calling all potential meaning into question (it is truly mysterious). So let me begin by considering the open book.

Purism

Charles-Édouard Jeanneret's *Still Life with Book, Glass and Pipe* (above right), which now seems an elegant but unremarkable painting easily mistaken for a Cubist work, was conceived in 1918 as an exact expression of the concept of Purism It also plays a key role in considering Ames' *White Compositions*.

In the mind and imagination of Jeanneret and the painter Amédée Ozenfant, their concept of Purism, if widely adopted, would restore regularity in a France recovering from the destruction of the First World War. In the paintings of both men (there were few followers) objects are depicted as standardized and reproducible *objét type*, or object type, including everyday items like bottles, glasses, plates, and musical instruments. In Purist ideology such object types had a moral, purifying presence. The main concepts of Purism were presented in their booklet *Après le Cubisme*, published in 1918. In the painting *Still Life with Book, Glass and Pipe*, 1918 Jeanneret wrestled with giving form to the idea of Purism. The open book is reborn in a number of Ames' *White Compositions*.

Judging from his writings, Jeanneret appears to have taken unreasonable pleasure in the violence of the First World War (as did several other major artists) because destruction could presage a new beginning marked by a new form of painting called Purism and a new order of reality, *L'Esprit*

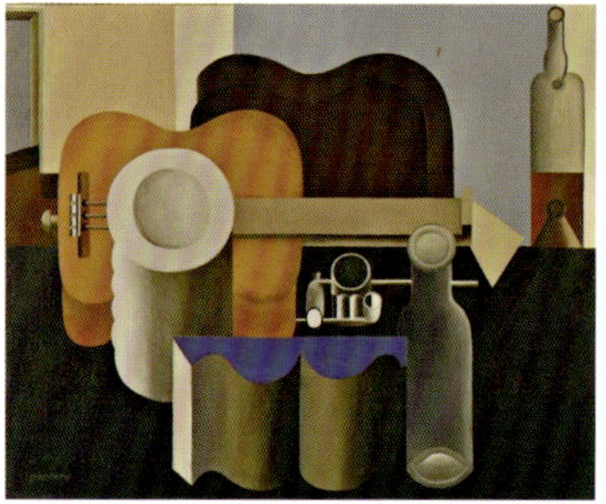

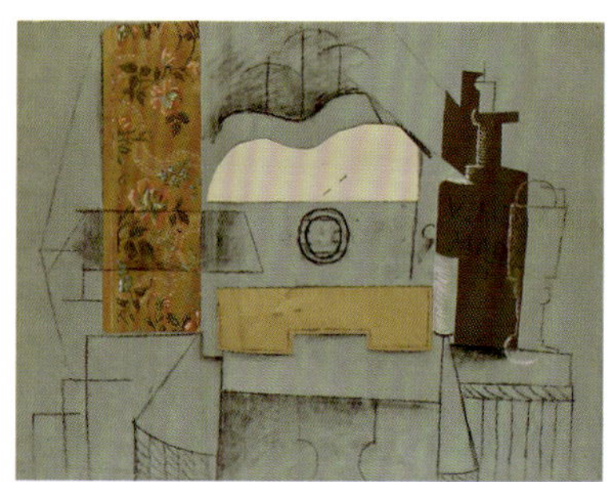

Nouveau. An intense need to purify reality must have been in the air in the first decades of the 20th century. It is present in Clive Bell's theory of significant form explained in his extraordinary book *Art*, published in 1914. He begins with the question, "What quality is shared by all objects that provoke our aesthetic emotions?" The answer, he writes, is "significant form," which he describes as "lines and colours combined in a particular way, certain forms and relations of forms, [that] stir our aesthetic emotions." (This statement could also be applied to all of Ames' *White Compositions*.)

I doubt that Le Corbusier knew Bell's theory of significant form, but similar ideas were present elsewhere in Europe. Before the First World War, and before Jeanerret became Le Corbusier, he worked briefly in the office of Peter Behrens in Berlin where he would have experienced Behrens's "machine aesthetic" and known the *Werkbund*'s advocacy for the *Gesamtkunstwerk*, or total work of art, that was applied to all the arts. He also would have been aware of the *Jugendstil* ideas of Hermann Muthesius, who advocated for *Typsierung*, or typification, the use of standardized designs that would be both suited to industrial mass production and reflect a uniquely German style. All of which seems to have fed into the concept of Purism.

Only a few days after the Armistice, signed November 11, 1918, Jeanerret and Ozenfant, published their statement of first principles toward new postwar aesthetics in *Après le Cubisme*, firmly relegating Cubism to the past.

"Cubism has become a decorative art of romantic ornamentism. There is a hierarchy in the arts: decorative art is at the base, the human figure at the summit. Purism wants to conceive clearly, execute loyally, exactly without deceits; it abandons troubled conceptions, summary or bristling executions. A serious art must banish all techniques not faithful to the real value of the conception."

In his 1977 *Artforum* essay "Purism: Straightening Up after the Great War," art historian Kenneth E. Silver writes:

"Alongside the image of reason and stability exemplified by Le Corbusier's Purist *Still-life with Stack of Plates* of 1920 (above left), let us put the futility and disaggregation that is the true story of the war and its aftermath. Working back from Purism toward the tragic disorder from which it emerged, let us go even further and plunge into the heart of the dialectic: in its origins Purism—the immaculate, hermetic art of Jeanneret and Ozenfant—is anything but pure. Its look, its iconography, its theory, its raisons d'etre, and its significance can only be understood within the physical and psychological frontiers of a brutalized and defiled France during the First World War. . . . Purism was a reaction against a reality almost too terrible to bear."

Silver offers a searing critique of Jeanneret's most ideological Purist work:

"We have only to look at Jeanneret's *Still Life with Book, Glass, and Pipe* of 1918, contemporary with the writing of *Après le Cubisme*, to see what this interpretation of history and art meant in visual terms. With only four elements arranged on an immaculate tabletop, Jeanneret announces the Purist entry into Paris and establishes himself in opposition to a work like Picasso's *Bottle of Pernod* of six years earlier. In place of the profusion of signs and symbols, printed matter, indications of inebriation, and an overall surcharge of information which characterizes the Cubist picture, Jeanneret's stark image of an open book with clean, white page[s] is a tabula rasa of the late 'teens."

He concludes, "Like the Purist book that cannot be read and the Purist guitar that cannot be strummed, Purist theory – concerned only with the construction of the well-tempered picture – appears to militate against its own significance."

Picasso's *Guitar, Glass, Bottle of Vieux Marc,* 1913 (above right) is a possible source for the Jeanneret painting to which he adds only precision and a book. If his driving intention was to show that Cubism was mere *ornamentism* he failed.

The belief that Purist painting had a moral presence that would benefit France may be absurd, but Jeanneret's passionate belief in the "cause" (and his central role in it) comes through in the intensity of his work. It could

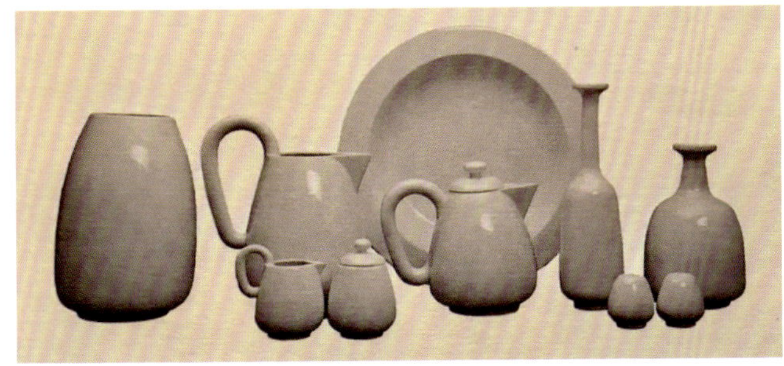

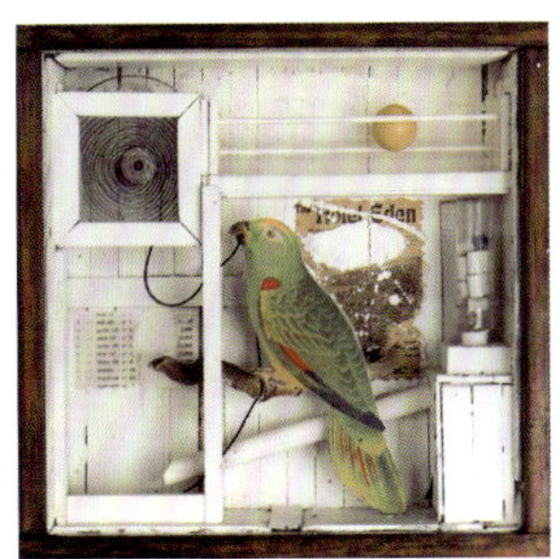

be argued that painting was a key step in the foundation of a modern movement that would transform the physical world, and Jeanneret, now calling himself Le Corbusier, was clear about his significance to it: witness his reply in a 1929 letter to a client asking for revisions: "The nub of the matter is this: I am the instigator of the modern architectural movement. All countries recognize this, apply my methods, exploit my ideas..." It must be noted that there were very few Purist works and that the Purism movement did not last very long, nonetheless Le Corbusier pressed on with his mission to transform the world. Of course, by this time he was delusional, but being delusional does not diminish the power of his artwork. Remember the stack of plates in all that follows...

In the catalogue for the 1996 exhibition *Object-Type Landscapes*, Ames offered commentary on Purism when discussing his own paintings:

"The paintings depict 'object-types' – general, yet specific, generic yet designed, familiar yet estranged. They are 'Purist' forms depicted in a still life landscape. The compositions employ overlap, convergence and diminution to imply depth resulting in the creation of the illusion of perspectival space. However, through the use of juxtaposition, superimposition and ambiguity of scale the perspectival effect is impaired. The result is a blurring of distinction between foreground and background that encourages a reading of pattern that reinforces the presence of surface plane. A dialogue is encouraged between the deep space and the shallow space – between the creation of implied space through perspective and the reinforcement of the surface plane though pattern. A multiple reading is fostered that rewards the careful observer."

This dense explanation reveals both what Ames gained from Purist painting and the critical process he applies to his painting scripture. His conclusion that "a multiple reading is fostered [in the resulting work] that rewards the careful observer" seems to me to be particularly true to gain the most pleasure from the *White Compositions*.

Around 1990 Ames created his own "object types" with a set of bold and stylish tableware inspired by the Purist forms of the 1920s (above left). In Ames' own words, the set was shaped "by notions of Morandi, a tangential cognizance of Chardin, and a nod to the vernacular .... [and] is at once designed and generic, modern yet timeless, simple yet elegant." There is no mention of Le Corbusier or Ozenfant, but these self-confessed Purist pieces play a role in many of the *White Compositions*.

White Compositions

So much for Purism. Ames is not interested in Le Corbusier as a savior but as a poet of form, someone who could imbue the simplest materials with a lyrical physical presence. This has played in his imagination over many years, thus these *White Compositions* offer a rare opportunity to experience objects formed out of decades of exploring a narrow set of themes. And although the work may contain an echo from the imagination of Le Corbusier, they are in every case built from objects and forms created by Anthony Ames.

The sculptor Brancusi called architecture "inhabited sculpture." In a sense I see Ames' constructions as architecture to be inhabited by the mind, to be read and enjoyed in the imagination. I have searched in vain for parallels for this work and view them as distinctly original. Though the connection is distant, I am reminded of the work of Joseph Cornell, whose boxed assemblages were created from found objects (above right). Ames' assemblages, some of which have the appearance of being boxed, are deliberately composed from recognizable objects that have a specific meaning or symbolic presence for him. Cornell's boxes have been likened to surrealist fantasies, and in a sense the Ames compositions similarly create formal yet surrealist puzzles for the mind. Like Cornell, Ames uses irrational juxtaposition, and though his pieces are devoid of sentiment, almost stoic, their effectiveness does derive from the presence of forms and objects that suggest a longing for a lost past. As much as I admire *White Compositions*, however, when compared with Cornell's creations, Ames' performances are so serious that moments of wit or whimsy are so subtle as to be lost to the casual observer. Again, it is multiple readings that reward the careful observer.

The Work

Ames' set of *White Compositions* clearly invites comparison with his better known paintings composed from many of the same elements.

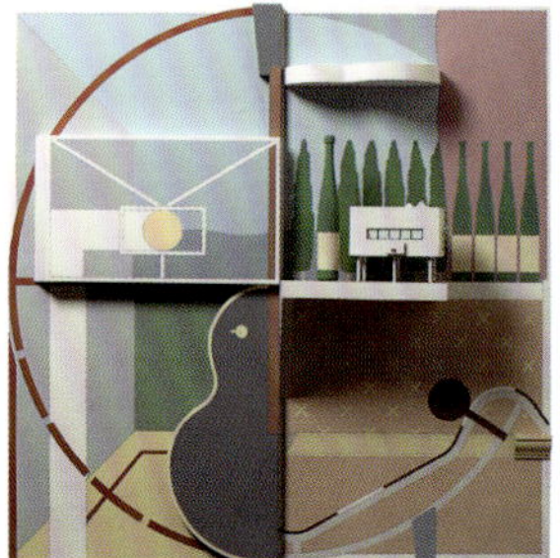

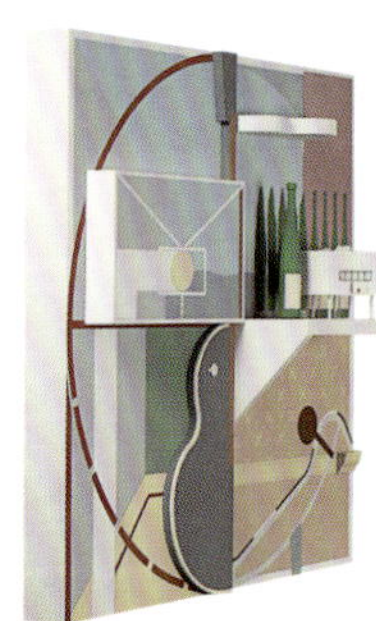

The paintings are complex entertainments filled with delight, whereas the relief sculptures have a more compelling presence: they are hard, clear and demand attention; they have gravitas.

The work, produced over thirty years, seems to fall into two distinct sets. *White Composition 1* to *White Composition 5* were based on or derived from painting, *White Composition 6* to *White Composition 12* were conceived of as sculpture. It may be that Ames moved to conceive of the sculpture independent of the painting because it offered more freedom. The result is that the earlier group of *White Compositions* is an extrusion from a two-dimensional composition, whereas the latter group is able to build narratives from a wider and more complex range of motifs.

In each of the twelve constructions Ames transforms the elements and proportions derived from Le Corbusier into his own language, resulting in intense, exquisite three-dimensional compositions. Identifying each element – vase, book, guitar etc. – does not interfere with finding pleasure in these dense and intricate structures, their pleasure lies beyond the literal interpretation of the collage in the way they entertain and puzzle the mind and eye. Of course, in enjoying the work we are free to offer our own interpretations, which will have no direct connection to the fictions from Ames' imagination. Unlike music, there is no need to play these works again to reveal their nature; they are always in the present to be looked at and experienced.

Garden Pavilion is the first panel where the elements are built on the surface plane (above left and right). They exist in contrast to, but harmonize with, the conventionally-painted panel on which they reside – challenging the understood 2D-3D reading of both. The title refers to a small studio/guest house, the Garden Pavilion, which the imagery reinforces. The romantic in me believes the architect was in love with this exquisite little pavilion and it was passion that moved it out of the painting into three dimensions. This was in 1990, almost thirty-five years ago.

The first three *White Compositions* are square formats that gradually begin to push at their edges in an attempt to contain their content. *White Composition 1* from 1995 is a masterly compression of the elements in the paintings that preceded it (page 30). A window shade and sectioned vase on the left side of the square are in danger of being consumed by a wall on the right. Ames describes it as "the first panel to go in total relief," which suggests he considers the paintings as panels. What Ames calls "mundane elements" – is this Purism again? – are arranged differently from the paintings, yet, Ames declares, "They still qualify as paintings – they are just painted white."

White Composition 2, from 1996, is a further compression and abstraction of the major motifs (page 32). It is a delicate, beautifully balanced composition in which there are a section of a vase, a fragment of the Corbusier eyeglasses, and a section through an open book. Adding mystery is a column buried in the mass of a wall. The choice of elements and their arrangement are arbitrary, Ames says, but the rules of composition are not. He writes, "The square, it's related lexicon of proportions – the swing down diagonal, the golden section, the double square, and the grid - all dictate rules of engagement that promote compositional regularity."

The third square composition, *White Composition 3* (page 34), made a decade later, in 2005, is the first to directly reflect a work of architecture, Ames' Martinelli residence. An extruded plan becomes a form balanced against what could be elevation details in the most literal – again, Purism? – representation of architectural elements and their relationships.

White Composition 4, in contrast to square compositions that have come before, is a hefty, rectangular piece of structure (page 36). It is from 2011. The concept of architectural mass suggested in the previous work now asserts itself and threatens to entomb the two surviving pictorial elements, a vase and drapes. A strange waving line from the drapes through the structure meets the massive column on the right. The composition is balanced by two small square frames, left and right, that bite into the wall, a square mass the same volume of the box frames, holds the middle. Ames notes that here elements both recede into the thickness of the surface plane and move out from it. In a sense, it anticipates the moves that he makes with *White Composition 5*, the piece made for the 2012 Venice Biennale exhibition.

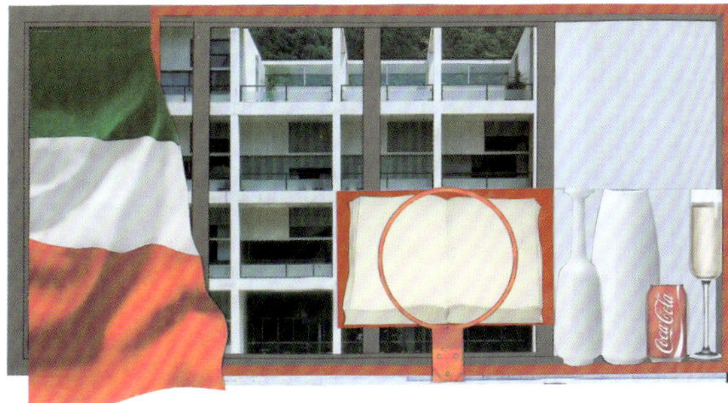

White Composition 5 (page 40) stems from a collage (above) in which a brilliant unfurled Italian flag flutters alongside Giuseppe Terragni's Casa Del Fascio in Como. The movement and color make the painting more dramatic than the white relief, in which the flag becomes a carefully hung curtain on one side and a red can of Coca Cola becomes a white cylindrical object on the other. Ames explains that the work was intended as a collage (recall the curators' mandate was to fill a box with things that inspire your work) that "grew into a white composition.The elements are the same in both [painting and composition] – a view from a sliding panel ribbon window, through a transparent basketball backboard with hoop, across a book stand with volume – to the Casa Del Fascio beyond."

Painting also seems to be behind *White Composition 9* (page 50), not from an Ames painting but Jeanneret's *Still-life with Stack of Plates* of 1920, which also appears to have influenced most of Ames' subsequent constructions. (I could be wrong but no matter.) Unlike the painting, in the reconstruction, space is flattened. The stack of plates (many more than in the painting) is placed in roughly the same location in relation to the guitar. Where Jeanneret's guitar form was repeated as a shadow, Ames appears to introduce a second guitar, a crude thing perhaps made from a cigar box. Ames runs the fret board of the simplified guitar body across the center of the construction. The wine bottle on the right of the Jeanneret is replaced by a vase of Ames' design. The rhythm of the stacked plates is picked up in the window slats on the right with a faint elevation appearing below the guitars. The two clay pipes at the heart of the Jeanneret painting are transformed into two eggs whose form is not unlike the bowls of the pipes. Although the reconstruction is overall consistent with the Purist painting, where is the book? It was the focus of Jeanneret's 1918 painting and the focus of Ames' work in the Biennale, yet here it is absent.

Variations on the guitar also appear in *White Composition 6,* 2022 (page 44), *White Composition 7,* 2023 (page 46) and *White Composition 8,* 2023 (page 48) only here,rather than running horizontally across the composition, the fret boards of the guitars become vertical elements that extend upward from a square frame. In *White Composition 6* the fret board and halved bodies of two different guitars divide the box into four discrete vignettes that become mentally inhabitable spaces. *White Composition 7* also divides the frame into four sections, this time with a single, if still half, guitar, a curious half opened book and the memory of the bowl of a clay pipe. Dominating all in the lower left quadrant is a depiction of Ames' porcelain jug with its splendid handle. White *Composition 8* repeats the general structure of *White Composition 7* with the same jug against an abstracted background.

In *White Composition 10* (page 54) all these elements come together in a complex composition comprising two framed scenarios, a square set on top of a rectangle. Again, the fret board of the cigar box guitar dominates and divides the composition. The open book appears in the square as if kept in place by the extended fret board. In the lower rectangle a small box imprisons a tiny Ames jug. The new and shocking element is the presence of a curved pipe coming out of the top of the upper box to suspend a lampshade, as if to illuminate the book below it.

The last "word," however, may be in *White Composition 11* (page 56) and *White Composition 12* (page 58), where the book that appears in Jeanneret's 1918 painting is the main element of the first composition, and in the second, a dominant element superseded perhaps only by the reappearance of that mysterious hoop.

All serious works of art must contain a least one mystery. In the case of the *White Compositions* it is the hoop. A clue may be found in a small gathering of men playing basketball on a Sunday afternoon at a suburban Y in Atlanta. Those who pause and watch the game would notice only one aging white man in this group of lively older players. From the behavior and the jokes and the criticism it is clear they've been playing together for a long time. And the aging white man is Anthony Ames.

Alan Balfour

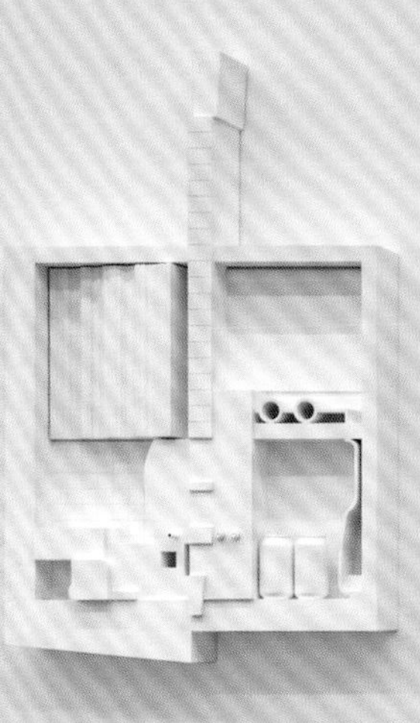
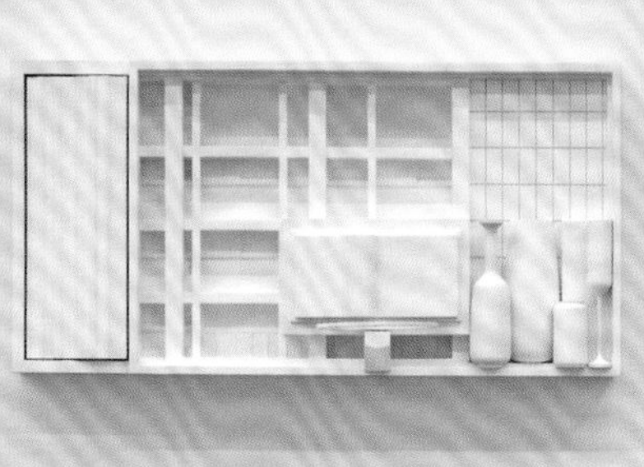
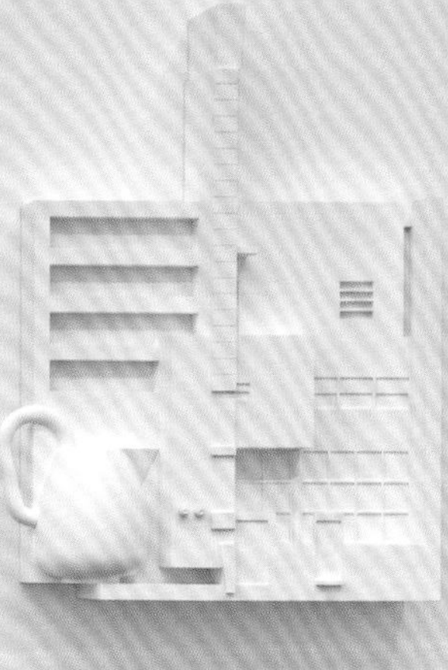

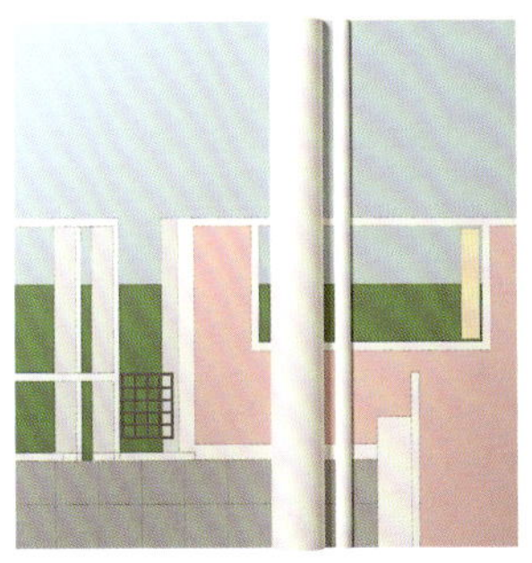

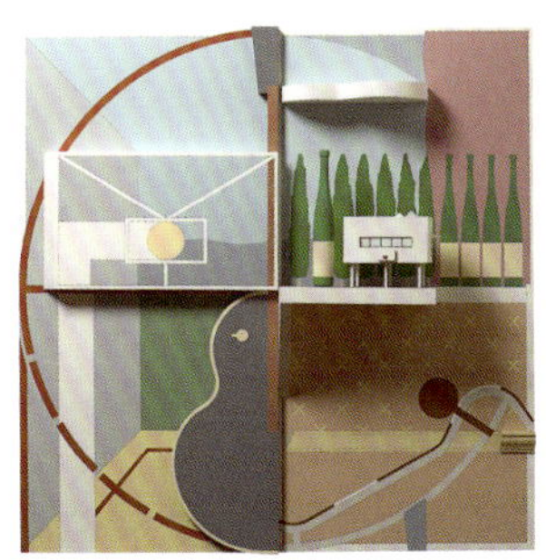

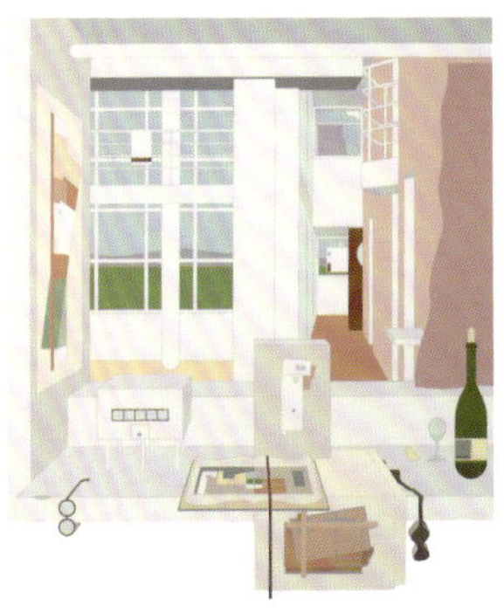

DOWN THE RABBIT HOLE

When logic and proportion
Have fallen sloppy dead
And the White Knight is talking backwards
And the Red Queen's off with her head
Remember what the dormouse said
Feed your head
Feed your head
-- *White Rabbit*, Jefferson Airplane

Some call them "Easter Eggs," but I like to call them "White Rabbits." They are the seemingly obscure thing placed nonchalantly in front of our eyes with the utmost intentionality: the hint or wink at a subplot, an alternative narrative that will come to fruition, if you're paying attention. Found in books, movies, video games, and computer programs, these are the breadcrumbs of erudite detail—the inside jokes and obscure secrets that pluck at our curiosity. I borrow the term from the psychedelic rock band Jefferson Airplane and the title of their song, *White Rabbit*, one of the most definitive songs of the 1960s. Grace Slick, frontwoman and writer of *White Rabbit*, declared that this groovy track is ultimately about exploring curiosity: following your interests down the rabbit hole by educating your mind through reading—"Feed[ing] your head." Among an amalgamation of references, Slick often explained her songwriting process as three thematic parts: she listened to Miles Davis' *Sketches of Spain* for 24 hours straight while experiencing an acid trip, she found rhythmic inspiration in Maurice Ravel's classical arrangement of *Bólero*, and she lyrically commandeered the story of Lewis Carrol's *Alice in Wonderland*. Through the layered composition of references and embedded thematic motifs (the "Easter Eggs"), I cannot help but make conceptual parallels between *White Rabbit* and *White Compositions*, a collection of 11 monochromatic relief artworks by architect Anthony Ames. To experience Ames' architecture, drawings, and artworks is to fall down a rabbit hole and emerge on the other side into a wondrous world: one where Le Corbusier, Michael Jordan, Bo Diddley, and Ames himself are all seated at the same proverbial table.

Through his precise craft and honed historical knowledge, each work by Ames is layered with allegory—including the occasional representation of an egg—a testament to his own intrinsic curiosity. Following his 2022 a83 exhibition, *Fifty Paintings*, Ames returned to the New York gallery in 2024 with a collection of 11 pieces along with a selection of related drawings. Simply named, *White Compositions*, this iteration of mounted works turns down the chroma and turns up the volume(metrics) with three-dimensional reliefs rendered in a uniform white. This new chapter in Ames' artwork builds upon five previous compositions, beginning in 1995 with *White Composition 1* and respectively continuing through 2012 with *White Composition 5*, adding six newer reliefs to truly forge a collection by 2024. It's revealing to see that the first five compositions are categorically listed on Ames' website as "Paintings," especially considering how spatial the compositions become when initially compared to the two-dimensional canvases. But like most of Ames' work, there's more to see here, more depth to explore; not all his paintings are flat, nor are they confined to the boundary of the canvas. Rather, Ames sneaks in three-dimensional columns that stand out of the picture plane as in *La Plata* (2016) (above left) or what could be construed as actual models in the painting, like in *Garden Pavilion* (1990) (above center). Through these procedures, Ames suggests secondary and tertiary layers—not solely of paint, but of poché—and objects that slip past other ontologies within the frame.

Tucked inside the dust jacket of Ames' first monograph, *Five Houses 1976-1986* (Princeton Architectural Press, 1997), there is a brief synopsis declaring this early volume as an "exploration of 'Modern and Pre-Modern space' through rotation, superimposition, and poche." A frontispiece opens the book—and his subsequent publications—with the various "easter eggs" Ames strategically tucks into each project (above right). A composition in itself, the detailed drawing depicts thematic objects and their dynamic moves, foreshadowing the motifs that appear throughout his oeuvre, visually communicating how to view and move through pictorial and architectural space. While the Modern influences are immediately legible, this notion of "Pre-Modern space" requires a detour into the typological history of, say, the French hôtel—where poche evolved, particularly in plan, to meet social needs propelled by cultural demands—or the Baroque garden, with its allure of theatrically forced perspectives and spectacle. Such meticulous techniques can be read in *White Compositions*, the packed poche of the hôtel (which

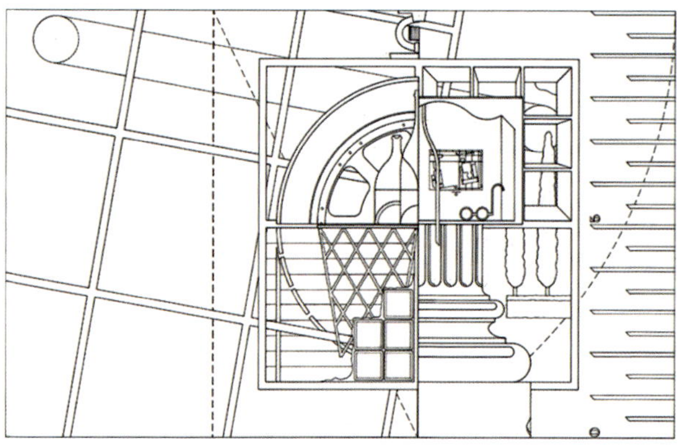

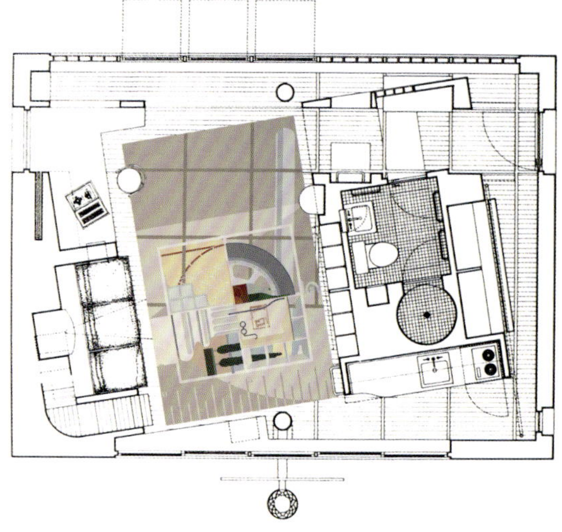

I effectively call the "box of chocolates"), and the placement of objects that keep our eyes and interest traveling across each relief.

While some have previously deemed Ames' compositions and their methodology "eclectic," I would prefer to celebrate their specificity as being inherently autobiographical, even bibliographical. Ames' arsenal of references weaves together alternative histories and reframing the modernist European canon with a very American perspective. Yet any fan of Ames will understand that the most delightfully complex references are the ones Ames makes to his own work, which harken polyglot designers, like Michael Graves, who traverse multiple mediums to challenge the status quo of what constitutes architecture—a tea set? its container? the building it lives in? This is the lure of Ames' compositions and the confluence of these motifs: the slippage among context privileges content. For example, the cover of *Five Houses 1976-1986* dons a white cover with a black line drawing not of a house per se but of a rug Ames designed specifically for The Garden Pavilion (above). The book cover/rug design begins to foreshadow details Ames embedded within the Pavilion, a coy riff on the Gardener's Lodge at the Villa Savoye with a basketball hoop below the ribbon window on one elevation—complete with a key in the pavement for real game—and a wink to the Maison de Verre's glass-block fenestration on the verso elevation. The play between form and history gives gravitas to non-architectural bits in the drawing: the wheels, hoops, glasses—of the wine and Corbusian variety—or, in basketball terms, its "swish!" Notably, the book's square format, a familiar shape that repeats within the *White Compositions*, means that the rectilinear rug had to wrap the book's spine. This subtle gesture already demonstrates the rules and how Ames intends to break them throughout the book and his subsequent works.

Similarly, the *White Compositions* attempt to negotiate these two shapes of the rectilinear picture frame, like the garden window at Villa Savoye, versus the square frame, as in the "blank screen" facade of Corb's Villa Schwob (the compromise of the two formats being the Maison Planeix with its extruded square volume punched with a rectilinear window on center). Ames further challenges both the static boundary of the frame and the logic of the disciplinary grid through pushing, pulling, or even hanging the objects within and beyond the picture plane. For example, the fretboard of Bo Diddley's infamous Gretsch "Twang Machine" performs as a regulating line, carrying its linearity throughout the composition then punches out of the frame; the curved handle of an Ames-designed porcelain pitcher hangs daintily off the edge of the relief. These gestures are reminiscent of deep-cut projects like Mies van der Rohe's 1923 Brick Country House scheme with its articulating walls, or Corb and Pierre Jeanneret's 1927 design for the Nestlé Pavilion, where seemingly gigantic milk product cans floated along the roofline. The *White Compositions* further challenge the notion of what constitutes a painting or a drawing, a model or a building. We may defer to scale to help us rationalize such objective categorizations, but there's more delight in surrendering to the surreal qualities of scalelessness, like Alice in Wonderland. These bite-sized architectures present alternative architectural realities into which I imagined occupying their spaces and objects. Gazing at *White Composition 9*, I feel the enormous scale of standing under the Swid Powell porcelain dishes stacked tall like the Capitol Records building in Los Angeles or plucking the Stratocaster electric guitar from a miniaturized version of the Villa Stein's facade (see *White Composition 9*). The compositions maintain two key qualities in each piece: the first is a determination to ensure the all-white objects are rendered not only legible in their plainness but also in their placement within each frame as they snap to a grid. The second quality is the use of anachronism and the accompanying uncanniness that ensues by placing objects in such close adjacencies, like the curved wall of the Galerie Tableaux in Corb and Jeanneret's Maison La Roche and the graphic large arc of a three-point line on a basketball court in dialog with one another.

Ames demonstrates how shifting the mediums can produce vastly different effects, even in the process. In his book *Fifty Paintings*, Ames divulges the incredibly precise process of his canvases: each panel is painted white, and the composition's line work is drawn, which also serves as a boundary for color application. Likewise, his design methods for *White Compositions* are equally fastidious: loose preliminary sketches proceed with a series of orthographic drawings, followed by a set of dimensioned elevations and sections. His series of construction documents, akin to those of a building, suggests that each composition is complete while acknowledging that architecture is not just the one-to-one scale object but rather the composed detritus of process. Ames'

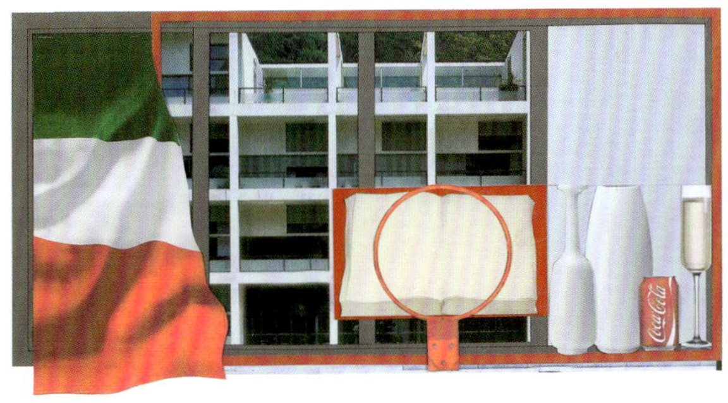

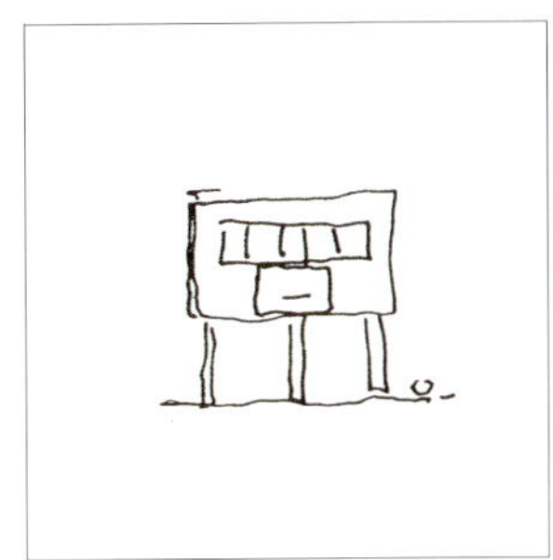

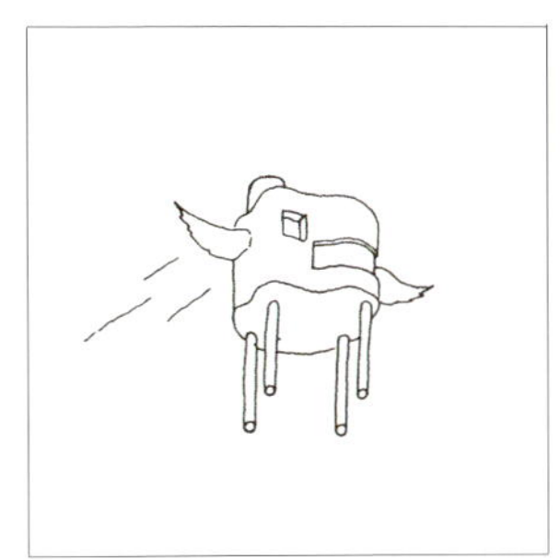

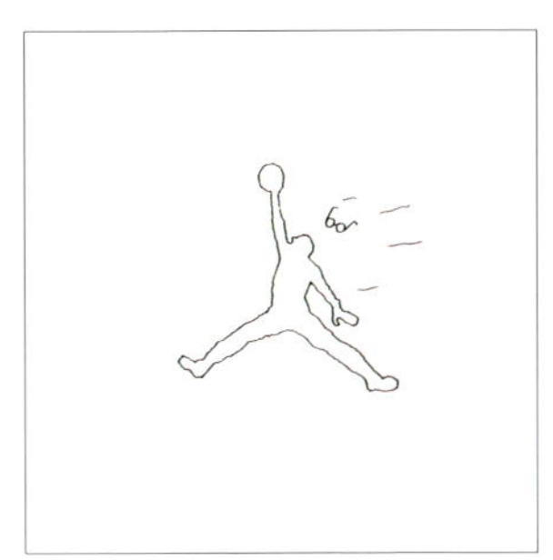

process for completion is demonstrated in the anecdotal fact that the oldest piece included in the show, dated 1995 and titled *White Composition 1*, was retroactively measured and documented—a testament to his holistic approach. Notably, this composition is the most demure among the 11 *White Compositions*—its volumetric articulation is simple, and the number of objects embedded within the relief is fewer yet as potent in their presence. This early version permits viewers to read the relief in numerous ways, from the projective to the prescriptive. Interestingly, the drawings help us further understand what we see—a key to the compositions—but never reveal the process itself, of what came first, of the first object down on paper or cut of wood. In viewing *Composition 5* on the gallery wall, the triptych relief reads as a commentary on facadism: a sinuous curtain on the left (the resolution to modernism's free facade), the Casa del Fascio with its phenomenal and literal transparency at the center, and the gridded glass-paneled facade of a standard curtain wall building. Superimposed on these facades is a basketball hoop in elevation with an open book as the backboard, along with a collection of vessels—vases, a soda can, and a champagne flute— that play with proportion and form. Hanging in a83's second gallery room, a hand-drafted elevation, plan, and section elaborate on the muted relief. On an adjacent wall, an accompanying collage discloses the details even further in full color: An Italian flag spills out of the frame to the left, and the Casa del Fascio's "billboard" serves as a backdrop for displaying Ames' porcelain vases, a Coke can, and a glass of prosecco (above left). Like its corresponding white composition, the collage is meticulously done by hand. Moving between these different forms of representation for the same object still requires an exactitude for Ames—like a lathe to shape the curvier parts. In a time of quick photoshopped jobs and 3D printing, it's refreshing to understand the craft and care that is poured into each piece. Moreover, each representational iteration defines the nuances between medium and scale—like an acoustic song going "electric"—it's more of the same, yet different.

White Compositions renders such dynamic spatial qualities between these objects, and the most compelling example of this is the only three-dimensional piece in the back gallery at a83. In this smaller, more square room, the only three-dimensional composition present hangs on its own wall: a single, cantilevered bookshelf with a tableau (from left to right) with a model of Maison La Roche, an opened book, a champagne flute, and a pair of those infamous Corbu glasses. The single shelf is reminiscent of the table surface that unfolds under the garden window at the Villa Savoye, a ledge to create impromptu vignettes with the landscape beyond as the backdrop. Mounted eight feet above the floor and four feet above the shelf is a basketball hoop in a matching white. It's austere, this tableau, and yet the details presented point to other references, like the "candid" photographs Corb staged at his various projects—as if someone had just stood up and walked out of the frame. I cannot help but notice the open book, its proportion echoing the trim size of Ames' own books and those seen throughout *White Compositions*. Despite its inherent blankness, I try to imagine which book it is and what page it's currently opened to. Yet the biggest gesture presented in this composition is that the frame is no longer restricted to merely hanging on the gallery's wall but has become the wall. The solitude of this composition—its placement in the flow of the exhibition and its location within the gallery—feels like the backmatter in Ames' books, where he always leaves the reader with a token: a small hand sketch. In *Five Houses, 1976-1986*, it's a sketch of his Garden Pavilion; in *Residential Work: Volume Two, 1986-2006*, the master bath volume from the Martinelli project sprouts wings and takes flight; and in *Fifty Paintings*, it's Michael Jordan losing his Corbusian eyeglasses while striking his iconic Jumpman pose (above). Hopefully, readers will also jump to the end of this book to see what "White Rabbit" Ames has left for us to return to, because his work always warrants another visit, another look, and will continue to pique our collective curiosity.

Courtney Coffman

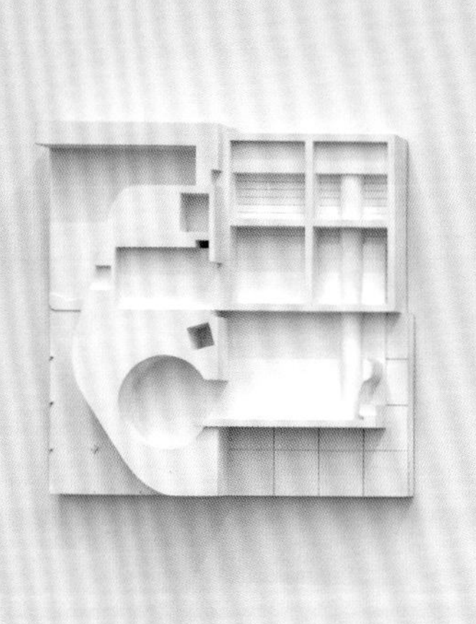

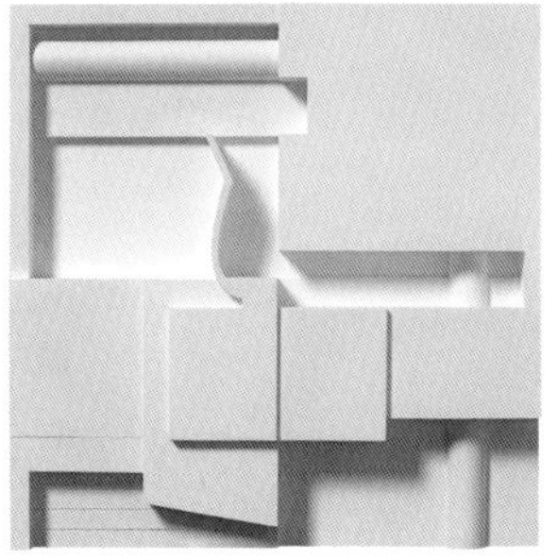

THE PROJECT OF ANTHONY AMES

Not until the middle of the fifteenth century in Northern Italy did painters realize that a painting could be more than the depiction of a narrative. This discovery fueled what would later become known as the Renaissance, a culture that aspired to a set of ideals that could now be projected in form and space. A dominant condition of this ideal was often projected on the facades of religious, public, and private buildings as a tripartite A-B-A construct. While such an ABA structure was the primary functional organization, it was also now iconic and symbolic. Both buildings and paintings of religious and cultural themes carried this now "classical" organization well into the nineteenth century, surviving such diverse styles as the baroque and the neoclassical.

When the dominant style needed to be replaced, the first attack was most often on the tripartite classical surface. Such was the case with the modern. By the mid twentieth century modernism had lost its supposed revolutionary fervor and had begun to champion the ideal of contemporary structure and function. It was here that architecture and painting split. Concerns for functional and innovative structures were mostly seen in architecture; they were not the problem of painting.

This brings us to the work of several architects today who still confront the problems of modernism, one of whom is Anthony Ames. Ames makes no pretentions about being avant-garde, but in his small three-dimensional collages, called white compositions, there is the unacknowledged attack on classical symmetry and tripartite composition. This attack is produced by collapsing the tripartite to what is commonly known in painting as the diptych – a two-part composition. And instead of an opening at the center – that is, instead of A-B-A – there is a frame or solid element that unites the two. It is difficult to think of "two" without a void in the center of the composition.

Beginning with his book *Five Houses*, modeled after the book *Five Architects* – both books being white squares – Ames has relentlessly pursued a career of formal examination that has lasted almost fifty years. With models, drawings, and collages, he has examined form between architecture and art, between collage and section. In his 2024 exhibition at the a83 Gallery in New York, he has recovered many of the tropes of his earlier work. But the eleven small white collages also seem to question those tropes. And whether consciously or not, the work seems to propose an alternate universe from any he has previously articulated. This is because eight of the eleven pieces propose some form of diptych; in other words, an explicit critique of the tripartite nine squares of Ames' previous work. Given the context produced by the twelve sectional squares, this new universe is a substrate of figure and frame and voided elements which implies a diptych, or four squares, as seen in *White Composition 1* (above). This condition of a central solid element is produced by both a void and an extension outward from the square ground in *White Composition 7* (next page). Another way Ames articulates a diptych is with the presence of figural containers – bottles, jars, and glasses (in both senses of the word). In several of the squares, a solid ground is replaced by a striation of linear elements which argues for two as a linear/planar dialogue. There are also figural voids that puncture a solid ground and, finally, the slight slippage of surfaces, which destabilizes the whole.

At its inception the modern project was a critique of ideality in both painting and architecture. But while it succeeded in critiquing painting, it failed in architecture. Why was this? Because of the difference in the two disciplines. Painting did not have to deal with structure or function, two requirements that the modern project in architecture had to valorize. And in that acceptance architecture idealized what it had started to deny. Fast forward to today. It may be possible to restart the architectural project now by reinscribing another trope, the diptych, as a critical tool to deny what has become a similar idealization in today's thinking about architecture.

The nine-square diagram is an archetype dating back to its introduction by Palladio in the sixteenth century, and the same nine squares defined most of the archetypes of the modern. If most architects feel that the period of modern energy closed sometime around the end of the postmodern, then Ames' late work can be seen as a search for the next conceptualist energy in architecture. In this context it is possible to articulate a new substrate or datum in the twelve compositions presented here; and that substrate is the diptych.

First, while Ames has made many paintings, it must be understood that

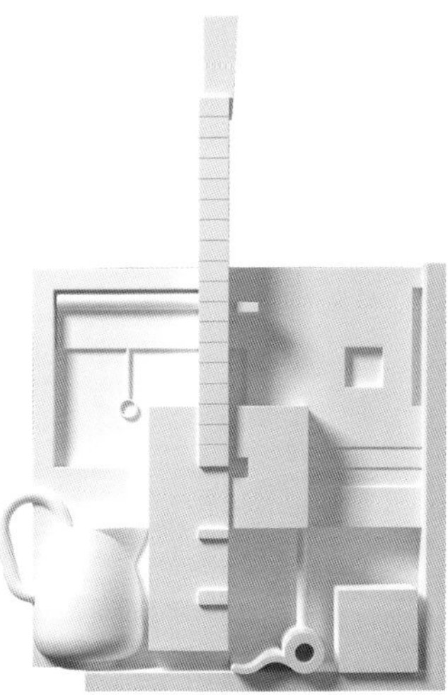

his project is less painterly and more architectural. That being said, the reign of the diptych has always seemed to fall outside of both the painterly and the architectural modern project. This is what makes Ames' work of interest today. First, it is essentially modern in its discourse, and it is precisely in the realm of academic discourse that both the modern and the formal are in eclipse. And second, it is his use of modern elements that produces the unsettled, ambiguous disturbances that puncture his collages which continue to cause us to pay attention. Only when they become too literally figural do they seem to lose our interest.

When the modern project became a banner of ideality, Ames moved to potential new narratives. Among these are the collages on display. When these are combined with the data bases of potential precedents, a new area of work will have been uncovered. The search for a new critique in architecture seems to be the aim of Ames' present search: a non-imitative formal project of the diptych.

Peter Eisenman

WHITE COMPOSITIONS

WHITE COMPOSITION 1

1995
ACRYLIC ON WOOD AND PLYWOOD
10 X 10 INCHES

This is the first panel to go in total relief. It was a logical 3D progression as elements on the previous panels (columns, window frames, door frames, etc.) were beginning to advance from the surface plane. Here again mundane elements such as books, a window shade, window frames, columns and a pitcher section are arranged and presented frontally and formally as they maintain a similar format as the colored panels. They still qualify as paintings - they are just painted white.

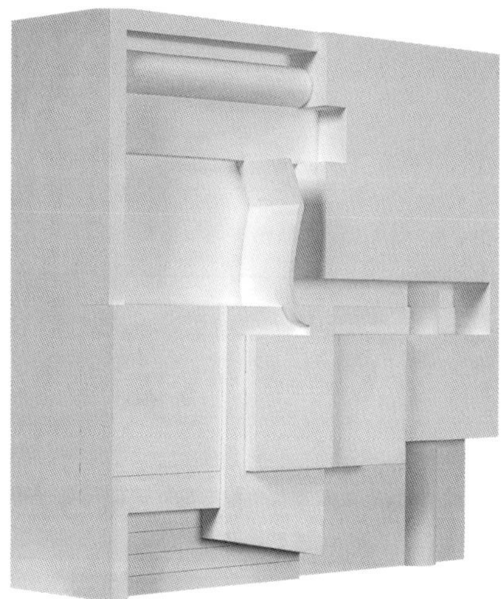

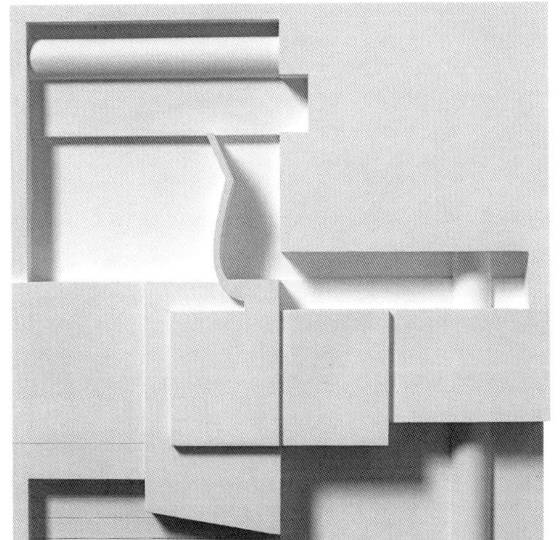

WHITE COMPOSITION 2

1996
ACRYLIC ON WOOD AND PLYWOOD
24 X 24 INCHES

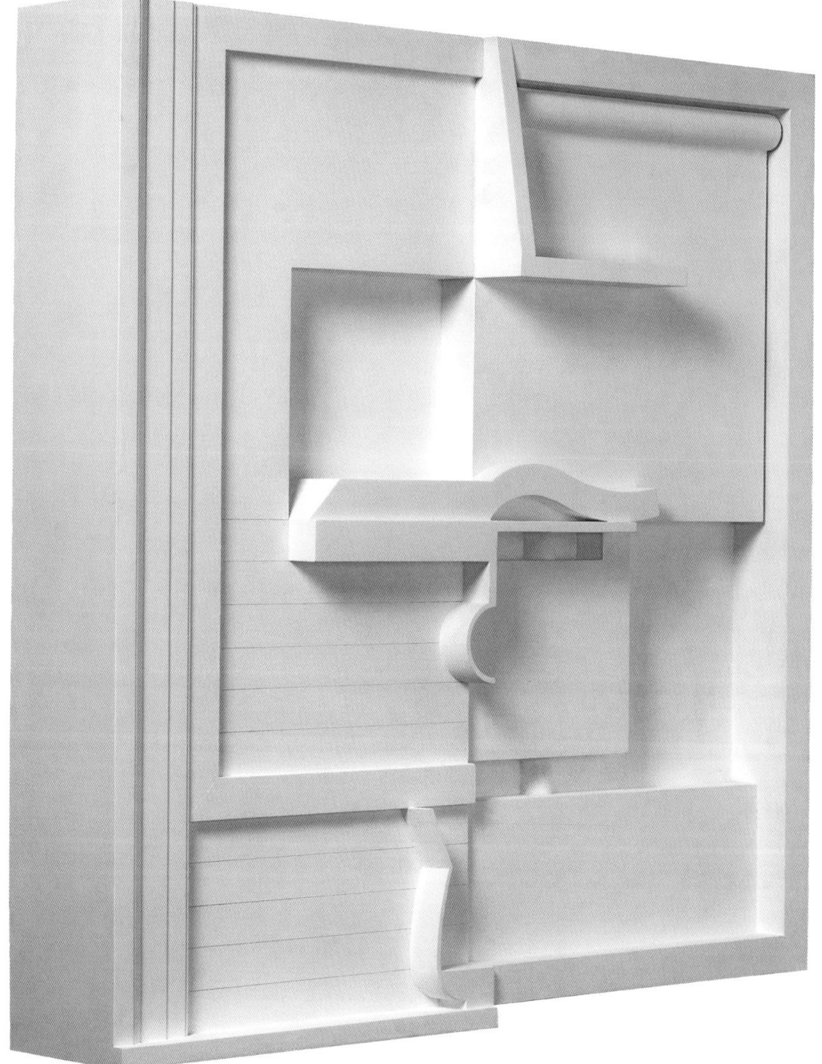

This panel, the second in relief, continues to explore the effects of the third dimension. The arrangement and choice of elements - although not arbitrary - is speculative. The rules of composition; however, are not. The square, its related lexicon of proportions - the swing down diagonal, the golden section, the double square and the grid all dictate rules of engagement that promote compositional regularity.

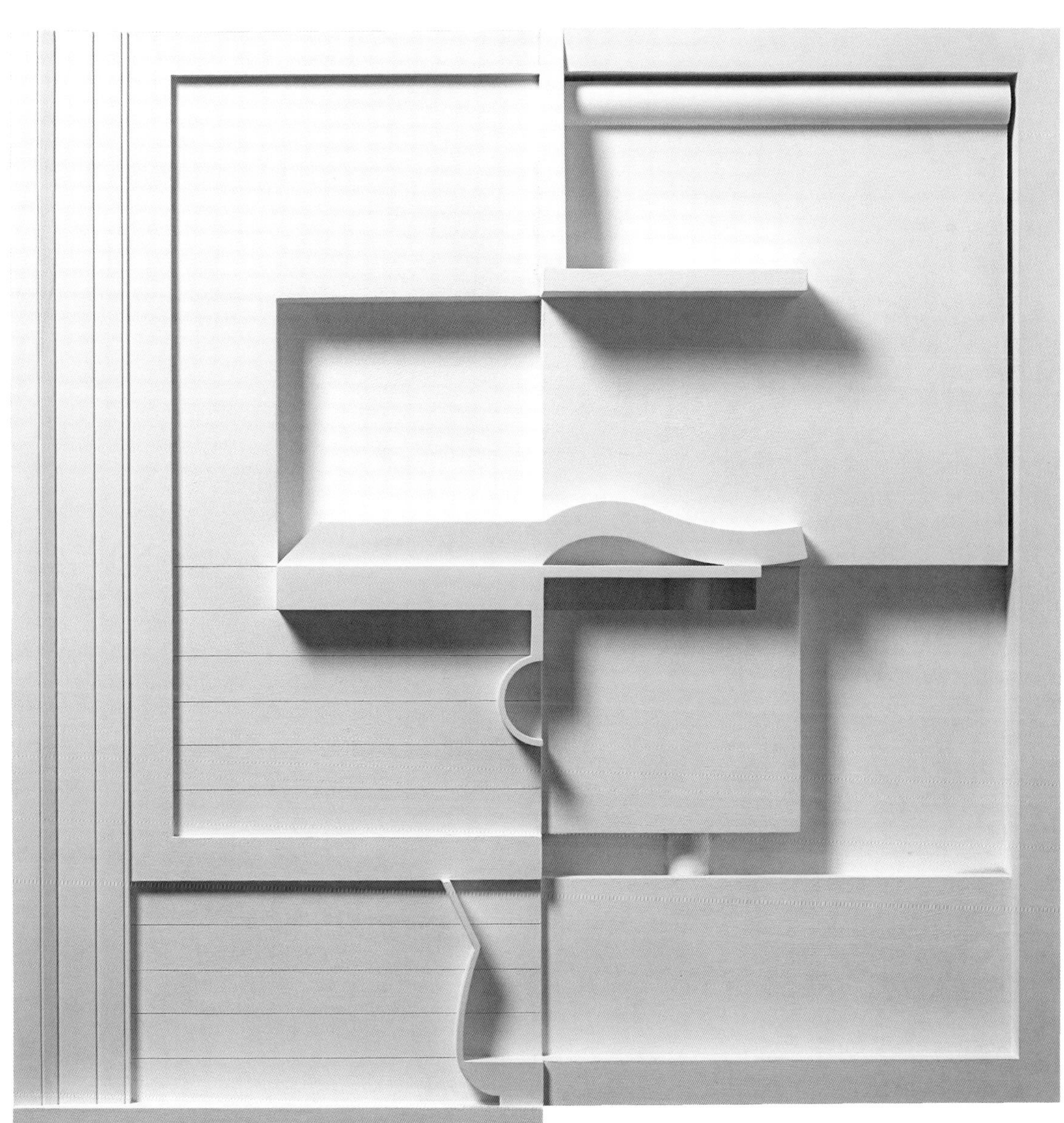

WHITE COMPOSITION 3

2005
ACRYLIC ON WOOD, PLYWOOD & COMPOSITION BOARD
24 X 24 INCHES
COLLECTION OF BILL LIPSCHUTZ

This panel contains elements from the Martinelli Residence. The left half of the composition extrudes a portion of the master bath on pilotis (below) while the right half composes architectural elements from the house such as a four-square window, a window shade, a column, gridded porcelain panel cladding, wood flooring, etc.

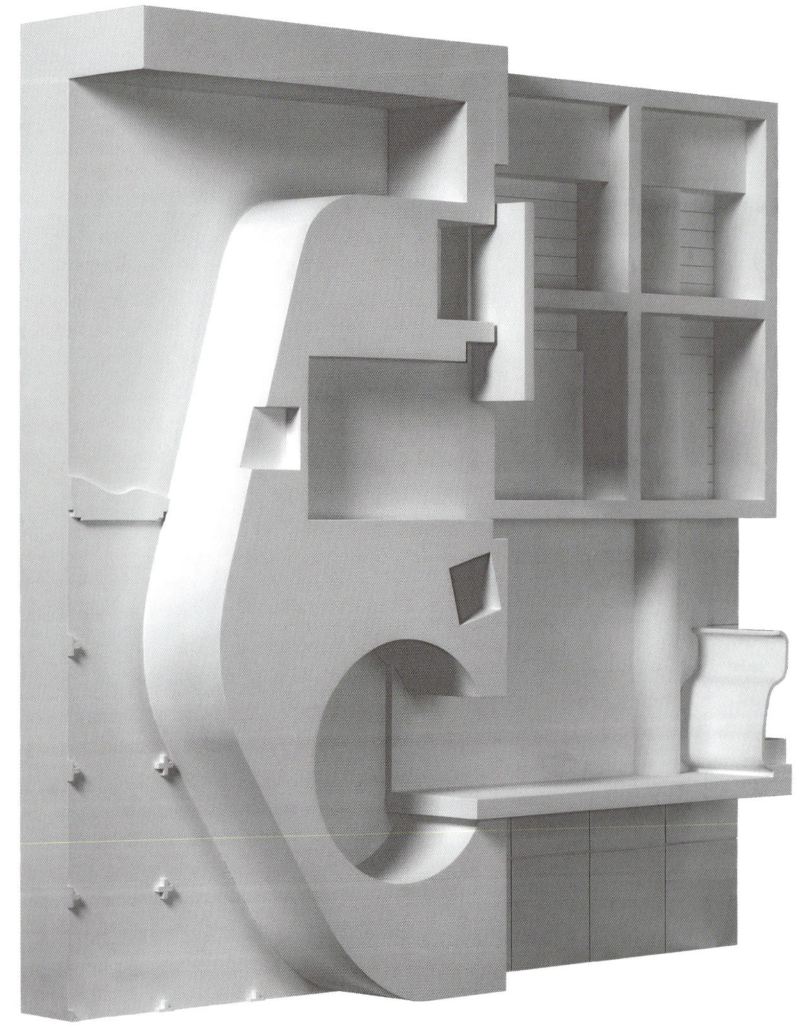

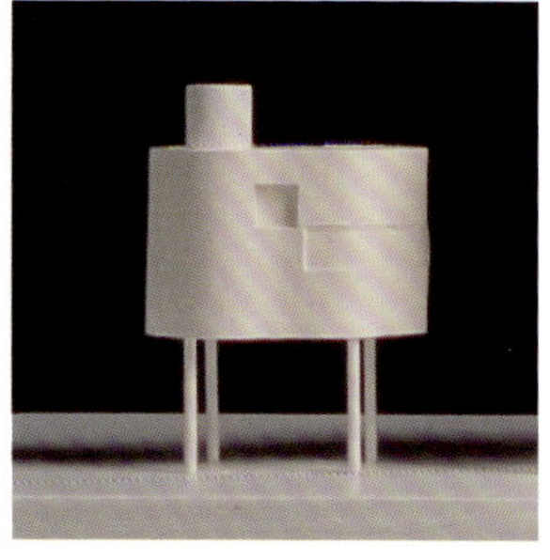

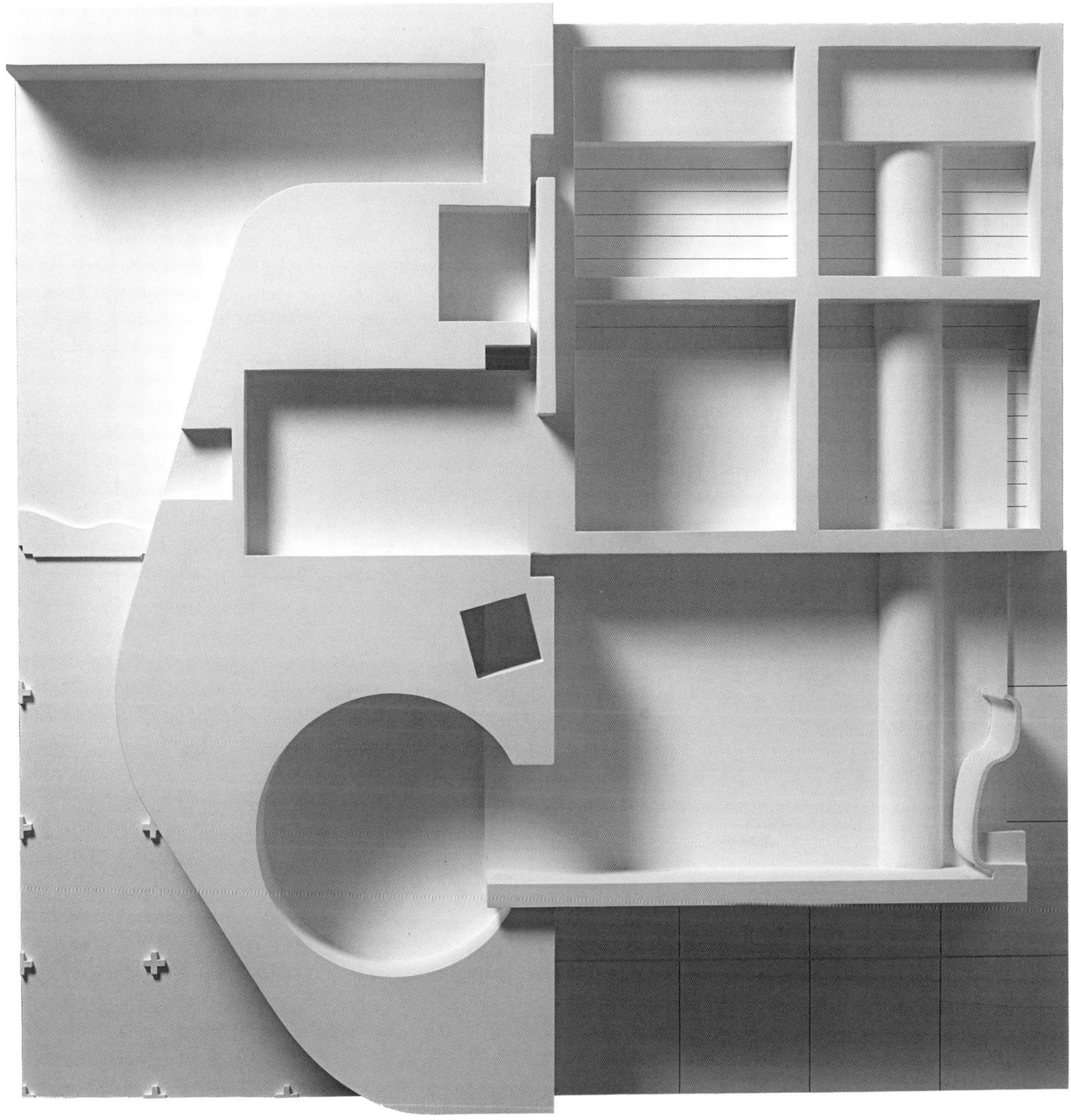

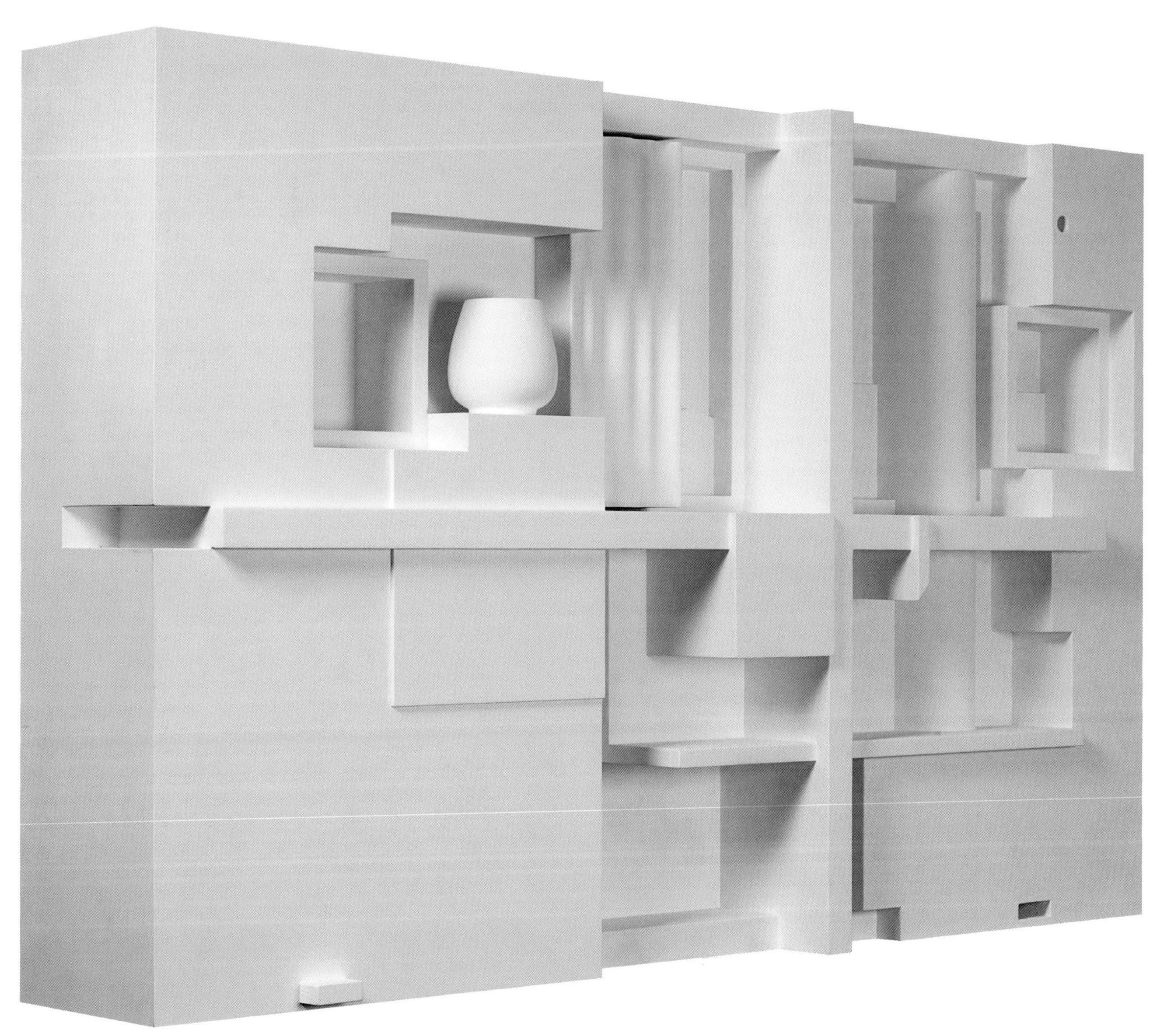

WHITE COMPOSITION 4

2011
ACRYLIC ON WOOD, PLYWOOD AND COMPOSITION BOARD
24 X 38.5 INCHES

In this panel we begin to explore an increasingly active interpretation of architectural form, space and order. Here the elements not only recede into the surface plane, but also advance from it. The emphasis on proportion stimulates the investigation while the apparent randomness of the selection and placement of the objects and elements appears to impair order once it has been achieved. The structure of the photo/collage below informs the formal strategy of the compositional diagram through bilateral and horizontal symetry, the placement of objects and the alignment of centers and edges. Also, both are golden sections with the left side of each defining the generative square.

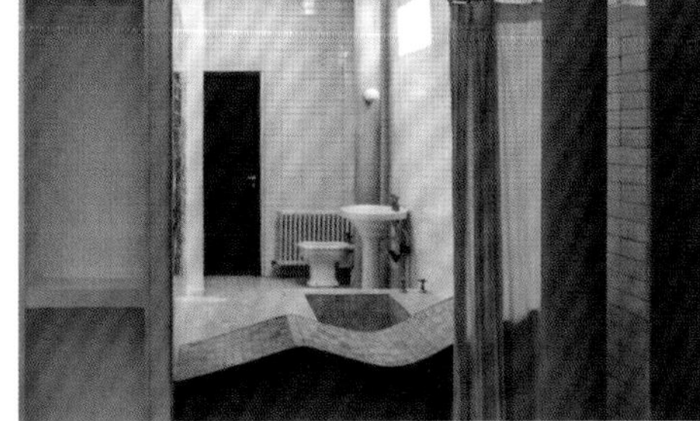

38

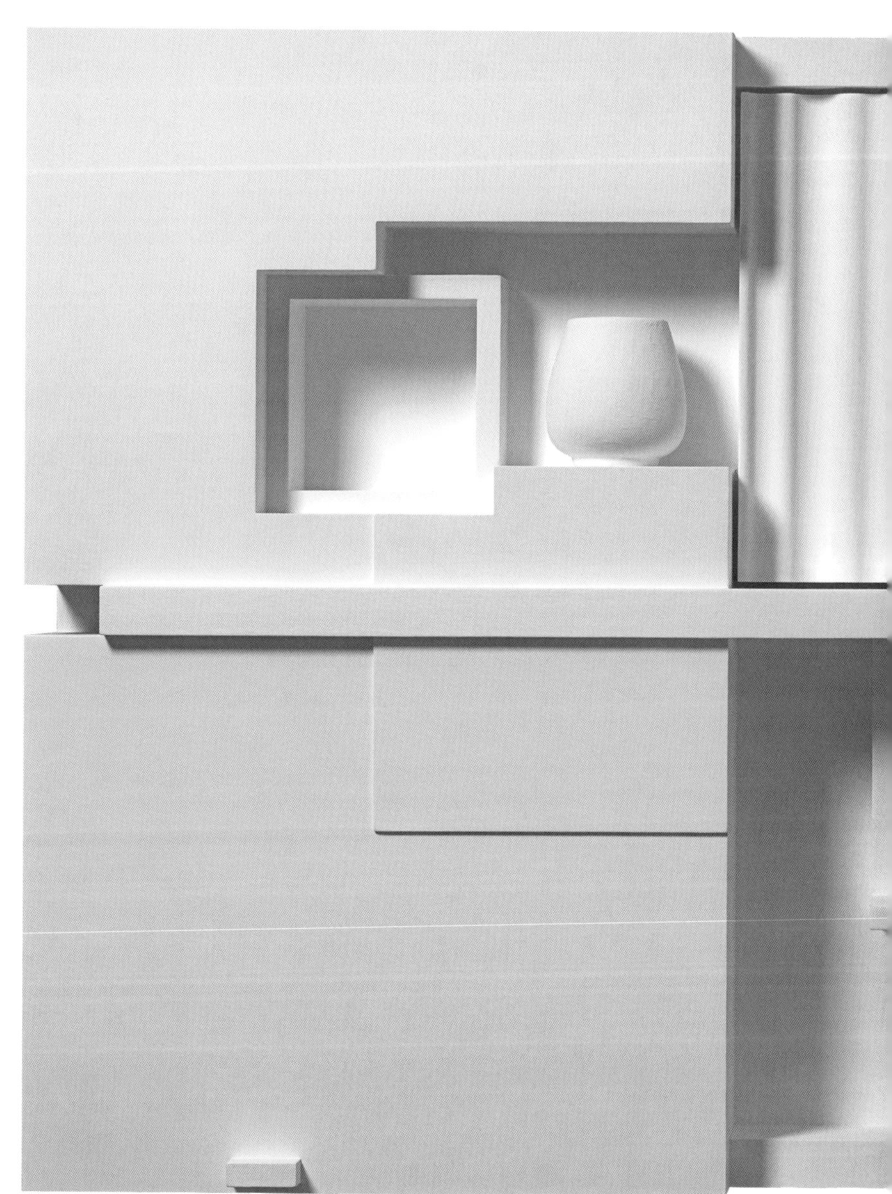

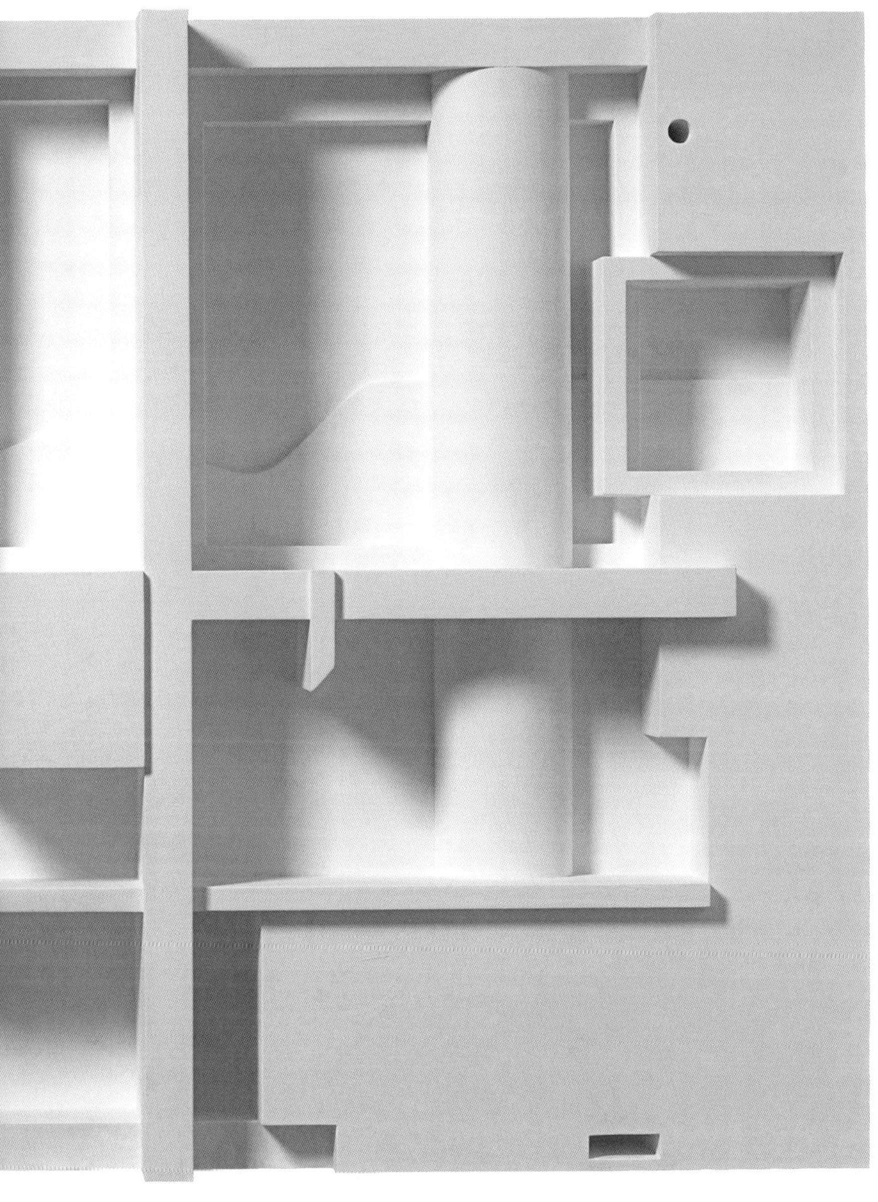

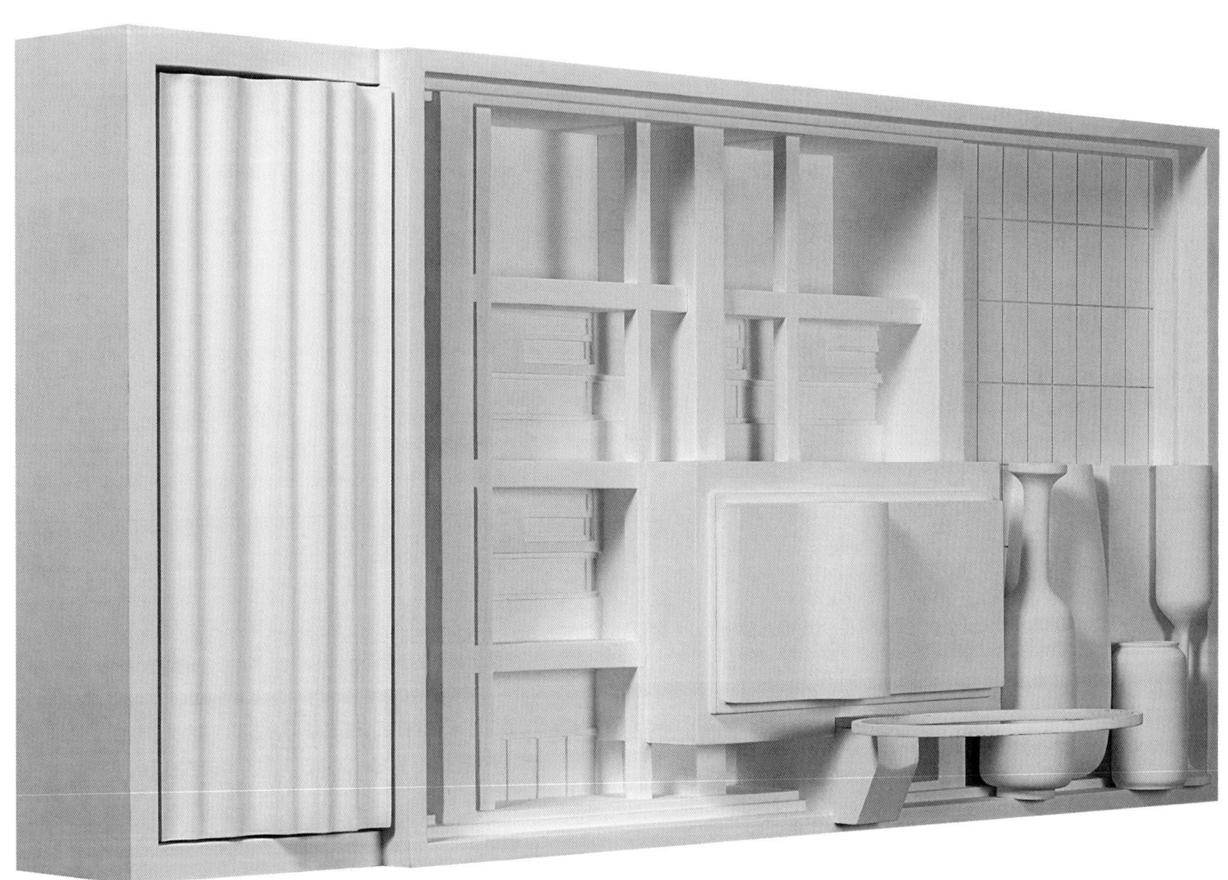

WHITE COMPOSITION 5

2012
ACRYLIC ON WOOD, PLYWOOD AND COMPOSITION BOARD
18 X 36 INCHES

This double square panel (opposite and following page) was originally composed as a collage (below). Subsequently it grew into a white composition. The elements are the same in both - a view from a sliding panel ribbon window, through a transparent basketball backboard with hoop, across a book stand with volume - to the Casa del Fascio beyond. An unfurled curtain is on the left and a group of containers is on the right.

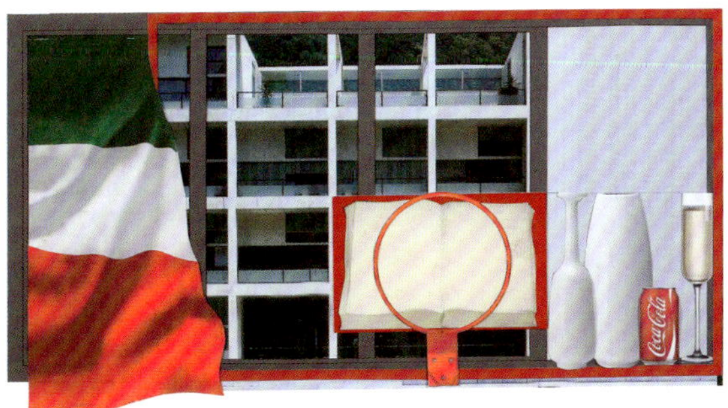

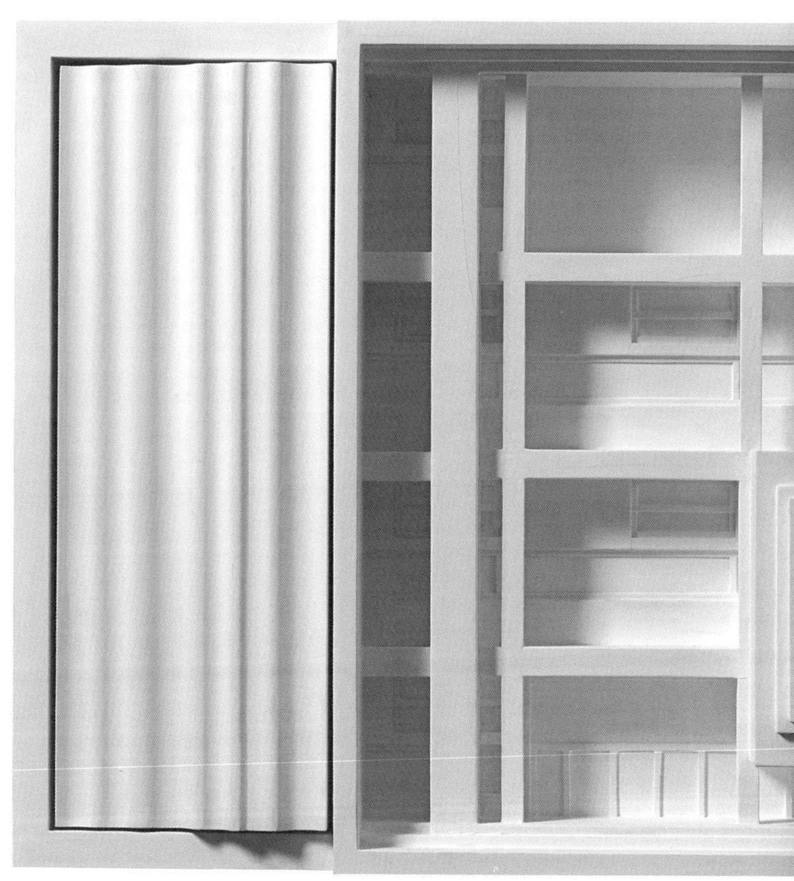

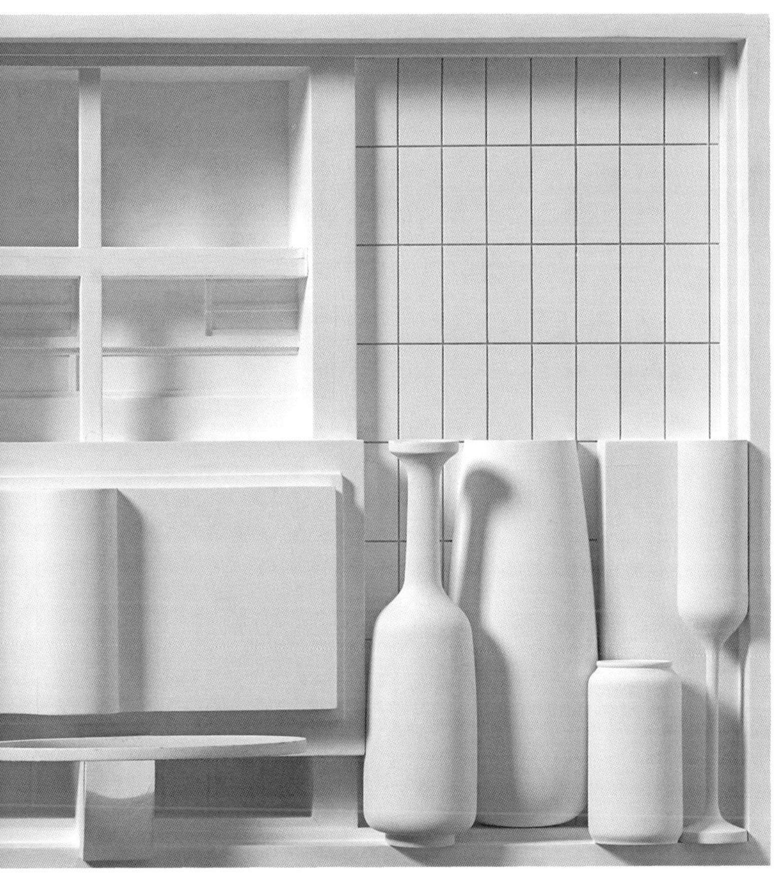

WHITE COMPOSITION 6

2022
ACRYLIC ON WOOD, PLYWOOD, ACRYLIC, ALUMINUM AND BRASS
38 X 24 INCHES

This four square composition proposes the assembly of not particularly kindred objects, but those more related through geometry, placement, alignment and obsession. One half of Bo Diddley's Twang Machine with its conveniently square cornered body is superimposed on the square. Its neck reinforces the centerline. Its size and shape begin to define and dictate other relationships - a curtain on the upper left, an adjacent shade on the right, the grid in the lower left quadrant, the center of knobs, chimneys, the top of soda cans. The lower left quadrant is occupied by Le Corbusier's 3D plan of Villa La Roche (minus Villa Jeanneret). It fits snugly within the square defined by the center of the Twang Machine, the bottom of the curtain and the edge of the frame. Nobody turns a corner, ends a dead end street or occupies a square like Corb.

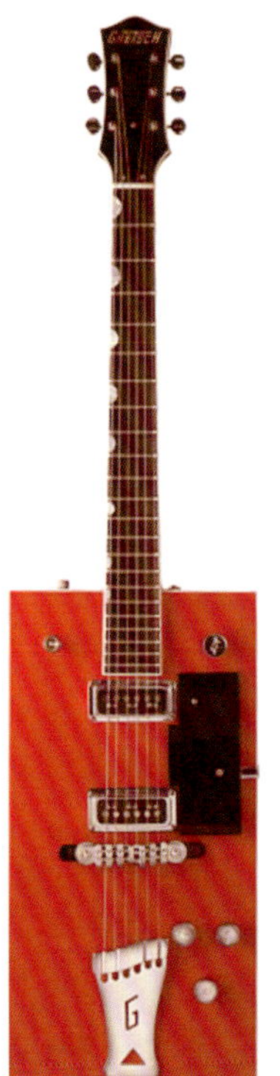

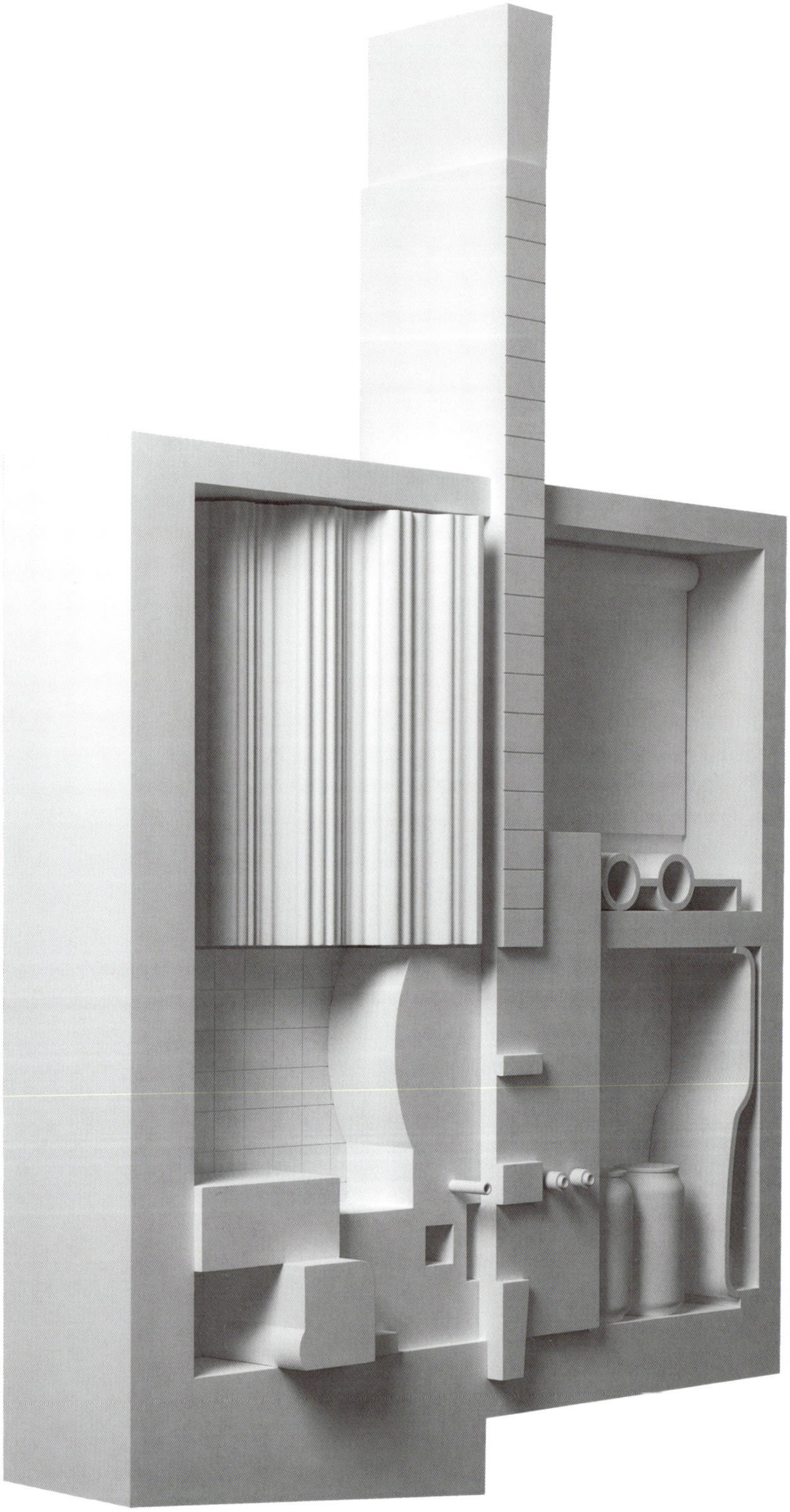

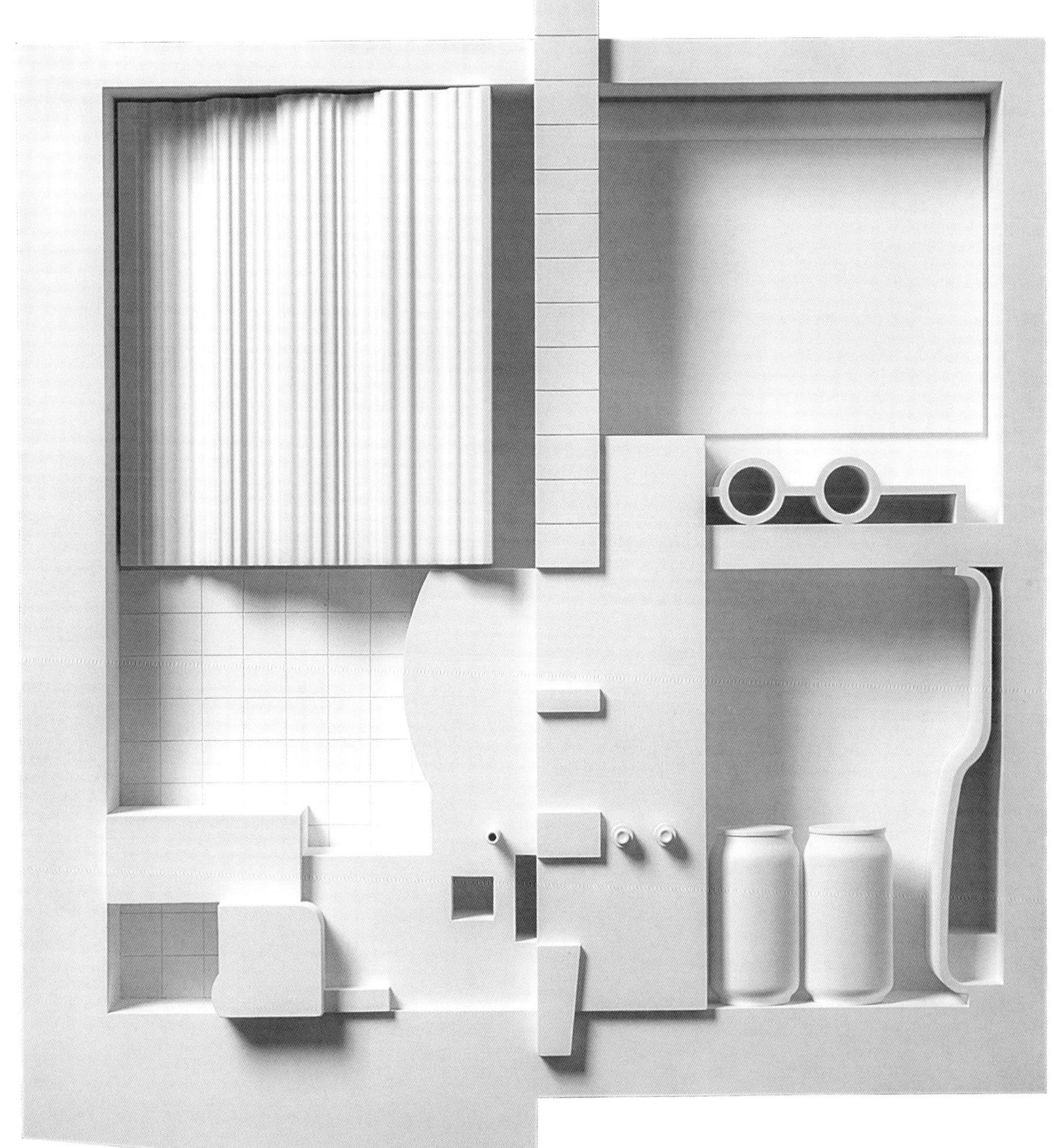

WHITE COMPOSITION 7

2023
ACRYLIC ON WOOD, PLYWOOD AND ACRYLIC
16.5 X 11.25 INCHES

A precariously placed pitcher - half on the shelf half off the shelf - in the lower left introduces a dynamic and perhaps an equilibrium with its handle extending beyond the boundary of the square compositions. This composition is smaller and consequently marginally simpler than the next one (page 48) - for which it served as a precursor. Consequently there is less detail on the guitar but more importantly on the entire right half where one half of Le Corbusier's Maison Planeix is appropriated.

Coincidentally the Maison Planeix was originally designed on pilotis and was open on the ground level as shown here. Like many clients, Monsieur Planeix did not seem to appreciate the purity of the "five points" and chose to clutter the lower level with garages, extra studios and other annoying poche.

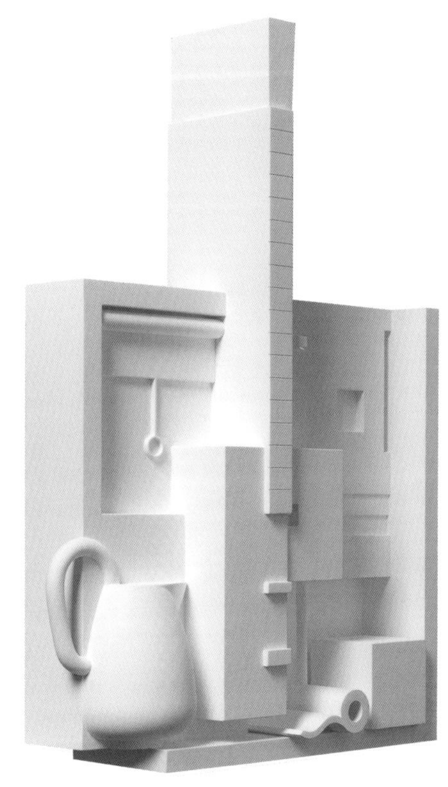

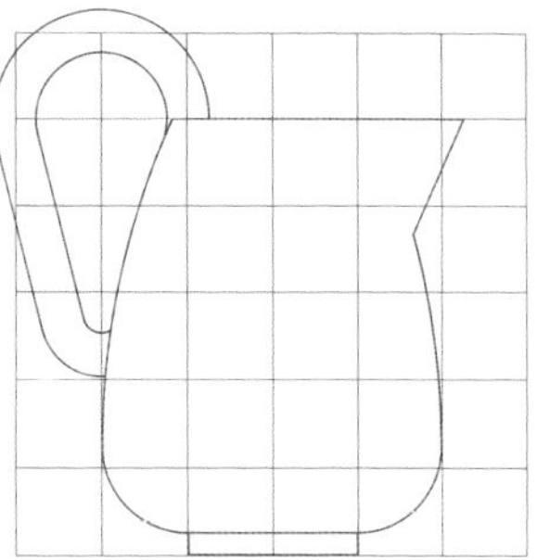

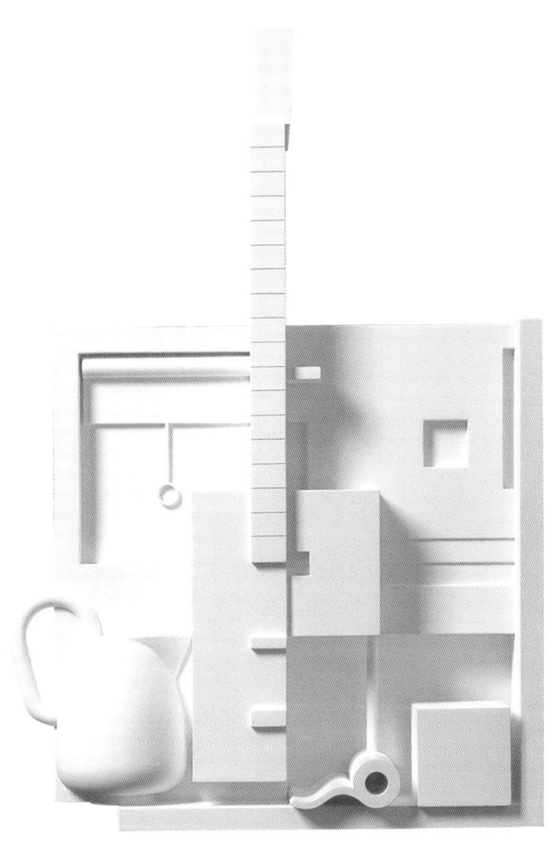

WHITE COMPOSITION 8

2023
ACRYLIC ON WOOD, PLYWOOD, ACRYLIC, URETHANE, STYRENE AND BRASS
37 X 27.5 INCHES

The Maison Planeix as designed by Le Corbusier is an exact square in elevation as is this composition. Within the implied four square organization the right half of it is appropriated and along with other appropriations it combines to generate an order and hopefully a harmony of disparate parts. Not incidentally the Maison Planeix employs a blank panel projecting from the facade surface. It is adjacent to the fret board and aligning with the top of the body of the Twang Machine.

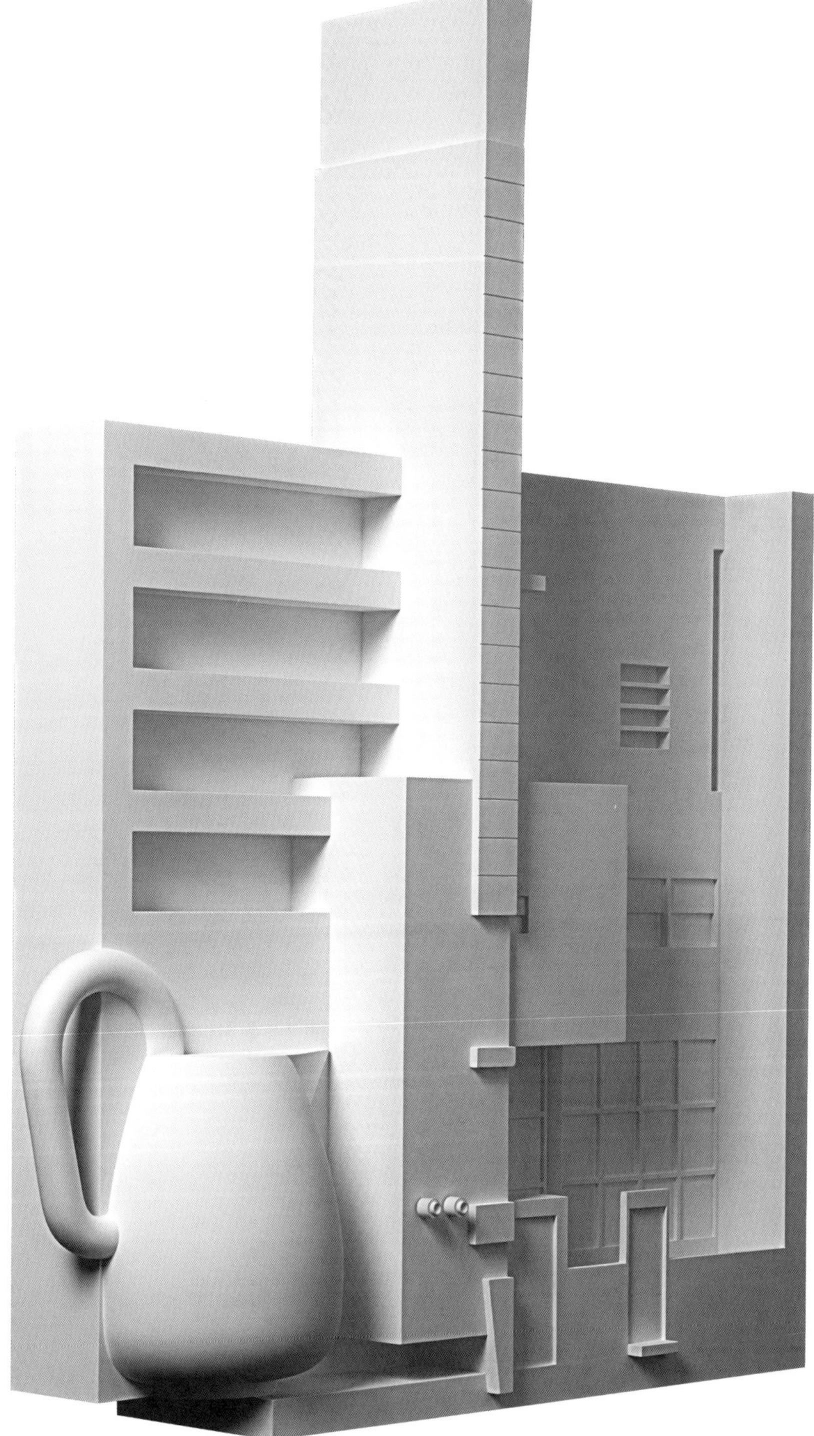

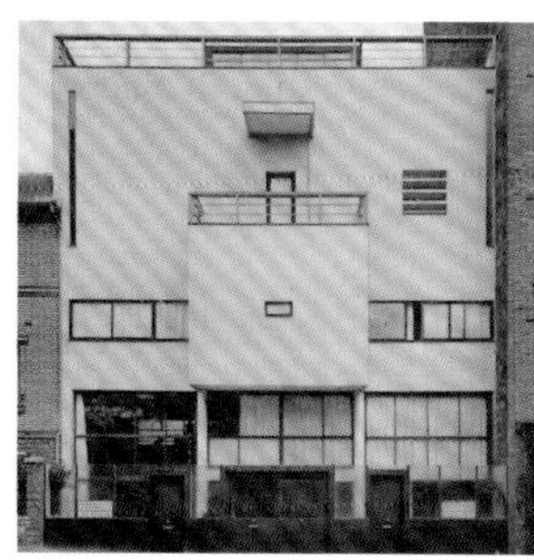

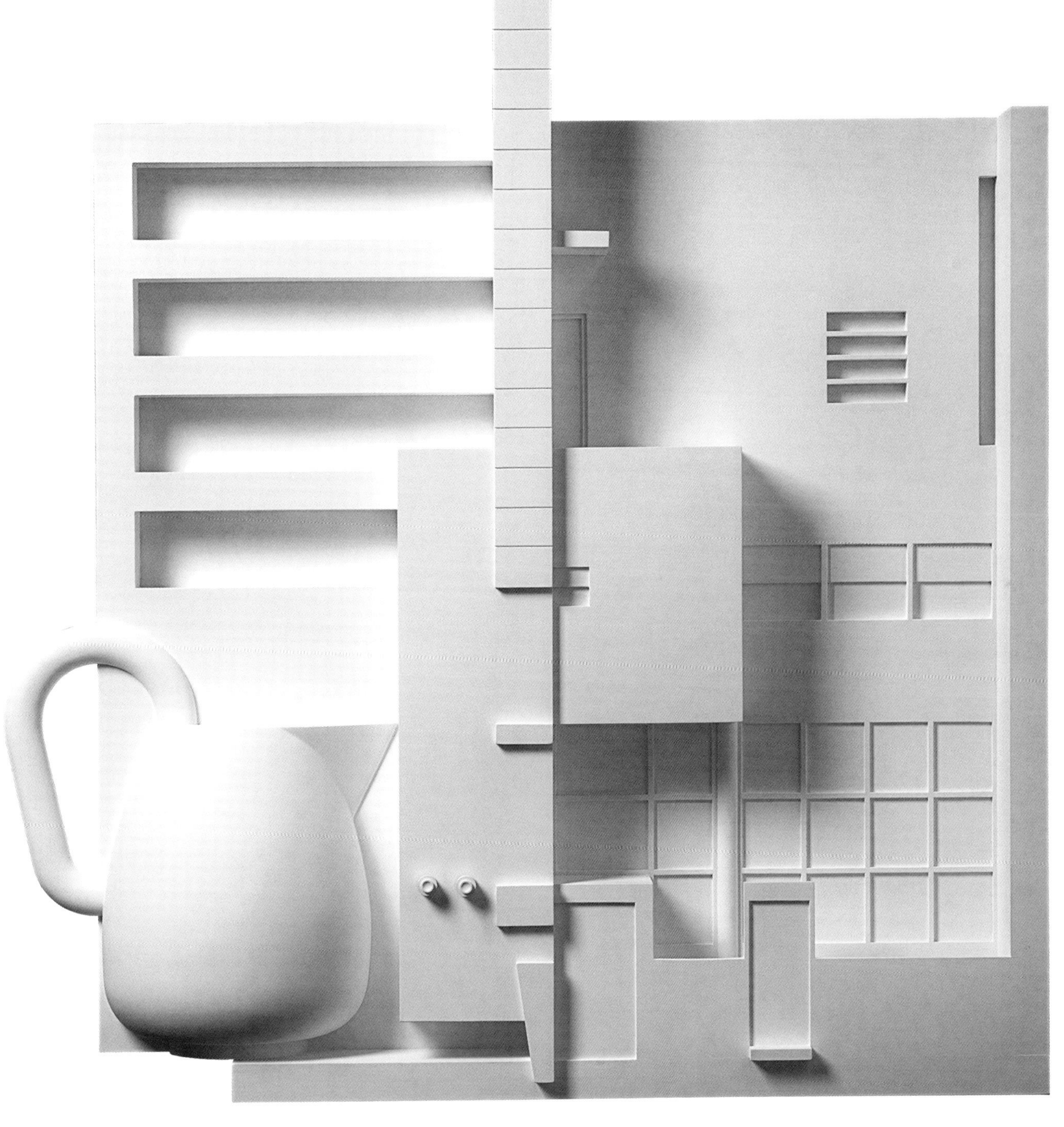

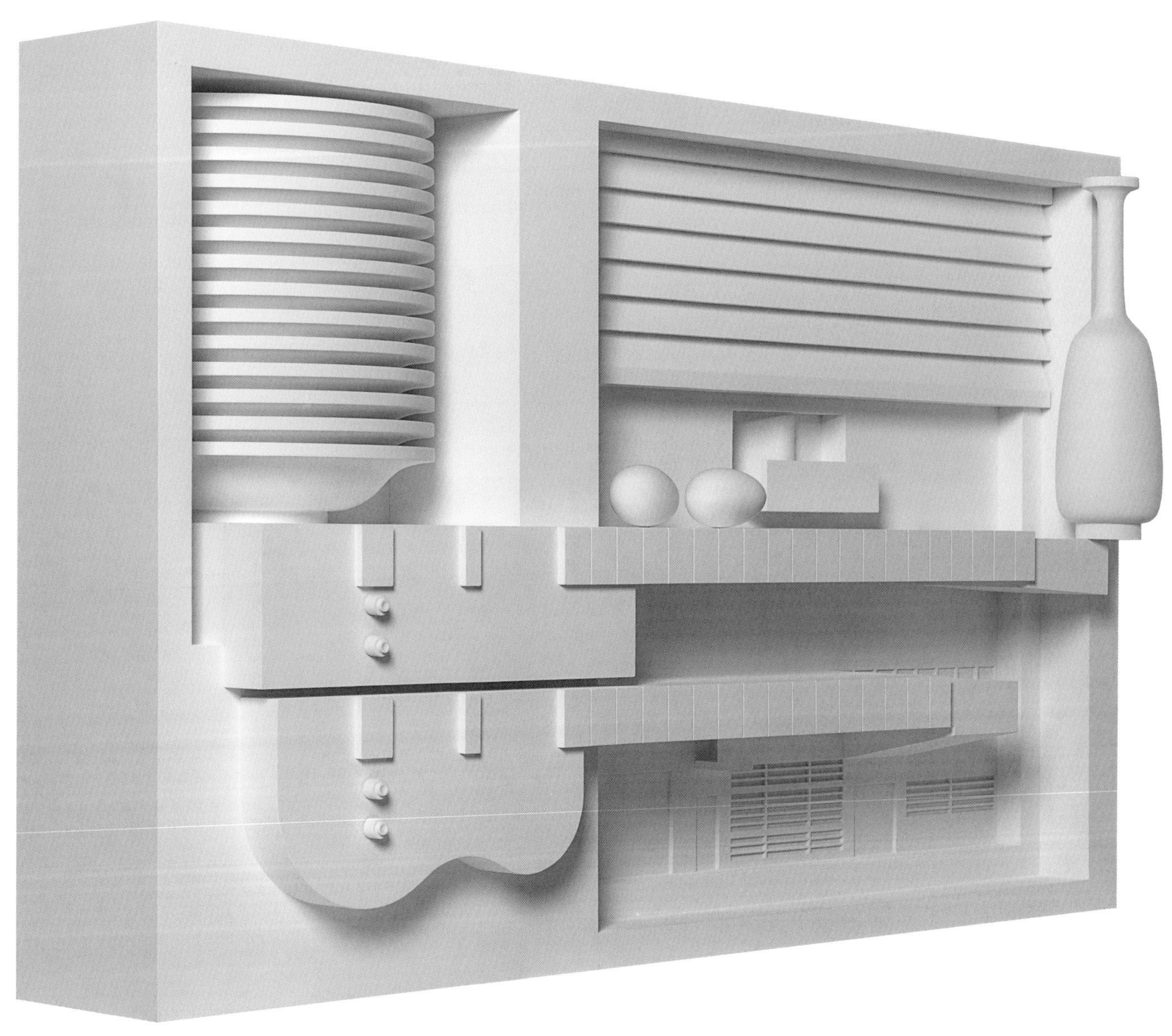

WHITE COMPOSITION 9

2023
ACRYLIC ON WOOD, PLYWOOD, ACRYLIC, URETHANE, STEEL AND BRASS
24 X 38.5 INCHES

The two guitars - Bo Diddley's Twang Machine and perhaps Joe Walsh's - which he played on his solo with Don Felder on *Hotel California*, the second best guitar solo of all time, or they may be read as Jimmy Page's double neck which he played on *Stairway to Heaven*, the third best guitar solo of all time - but I digress. Both guitar necks are superimposed on the ribbon windows at Villa Stein which can be seen out of the window beneath the venetian blind. The vase and stacked bowls make reference to and were appropriated from Corb's Purist painting *Still-life with Stack of Plates*, 1920 (below). The two eggs are a conceit - one of which marks center.

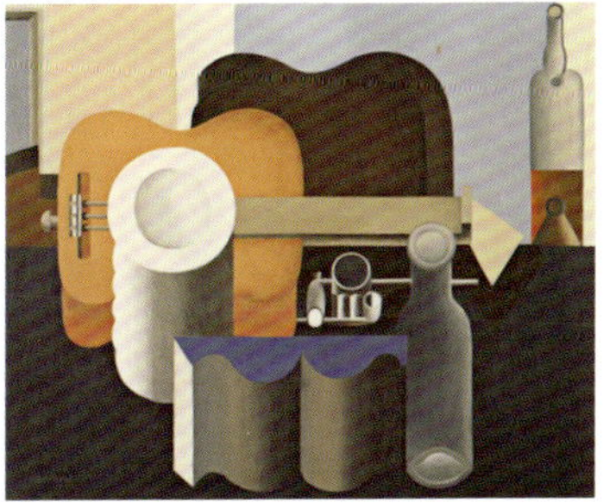

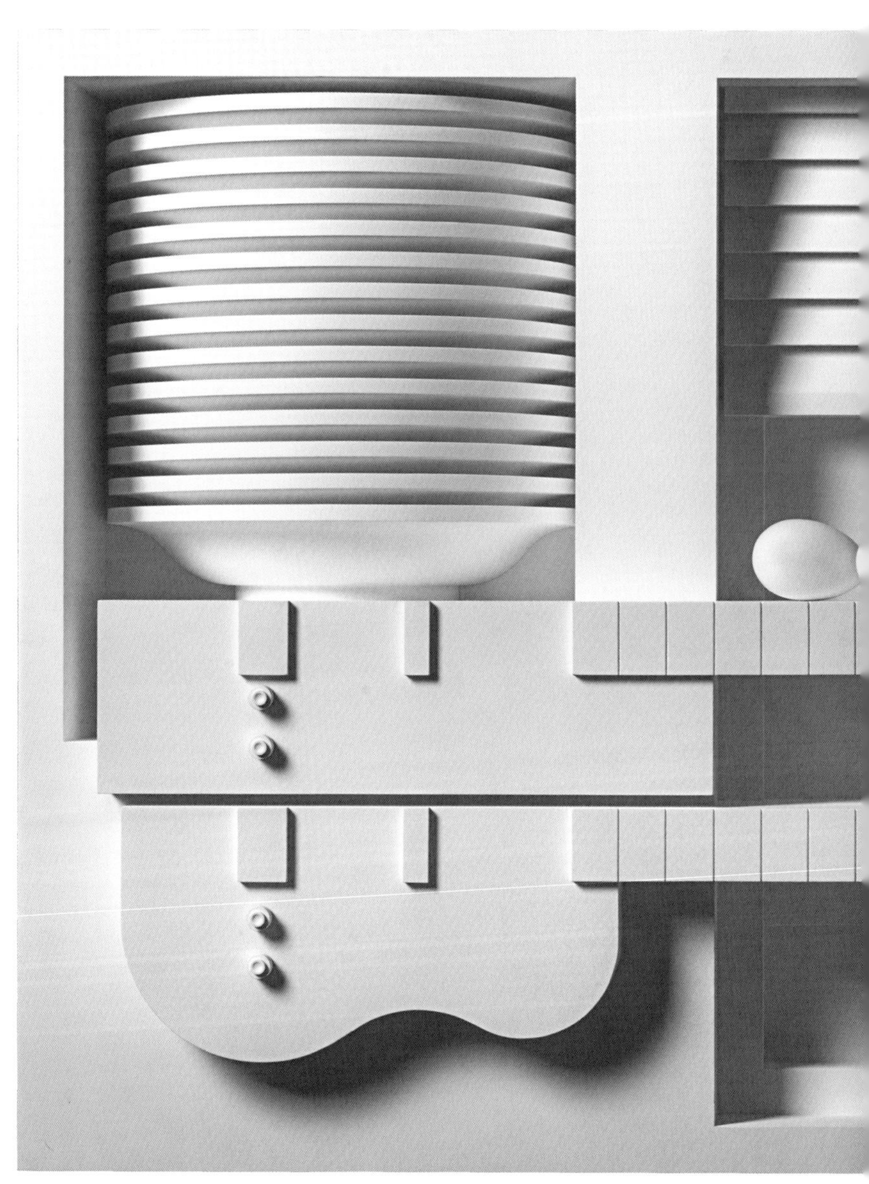

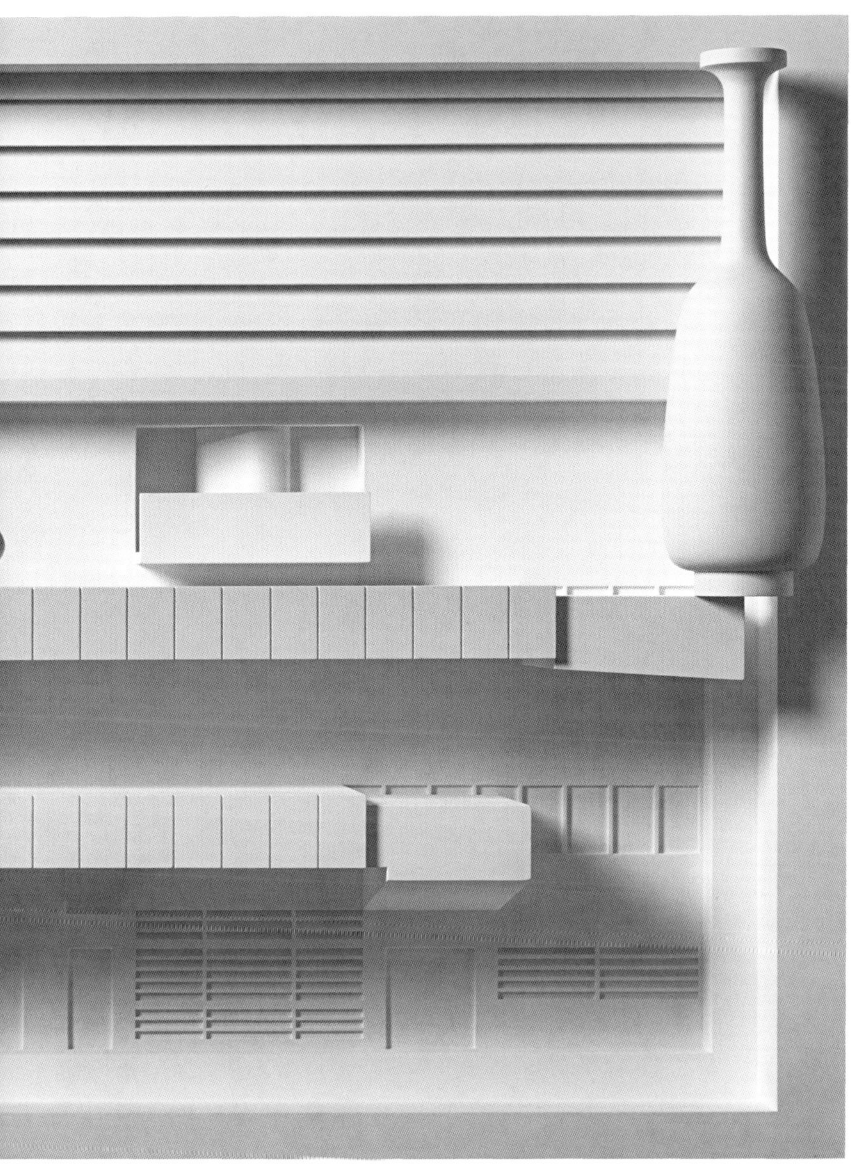

WHITE COMPOSITION 10

2024
ACRYLIC ON WOOD, PLYWOOD, PVC, STEEL, URETHANE AND POLYCARBONATE
41 X 29 INCHES

The open frame and its close cousin the blank panel have long been tropes or leitmotifs in the practice of architecture - from the open frame on Chiesa di San Marcello al Corso in Rome (bottom left) to the blank panel on Le Corbusier's Villa Schwob (bottom right).

The shape of this composition is formal and simple employing a square frame and a golden section rectangle that it generates. The top frame may be read as a window with a shade and an open book obscuring the view. The bottom frame proposes a framed transparent basketball backboard with a rectangle target and a hoop attached. It also contains a shade. A pitcher resides within the recessed rectangular target above the rim. A goose neck industrial light fixture and the ubiquitous basketball rim mark the center of this diptych. The edge of the neck of the Twang Machine holds it.

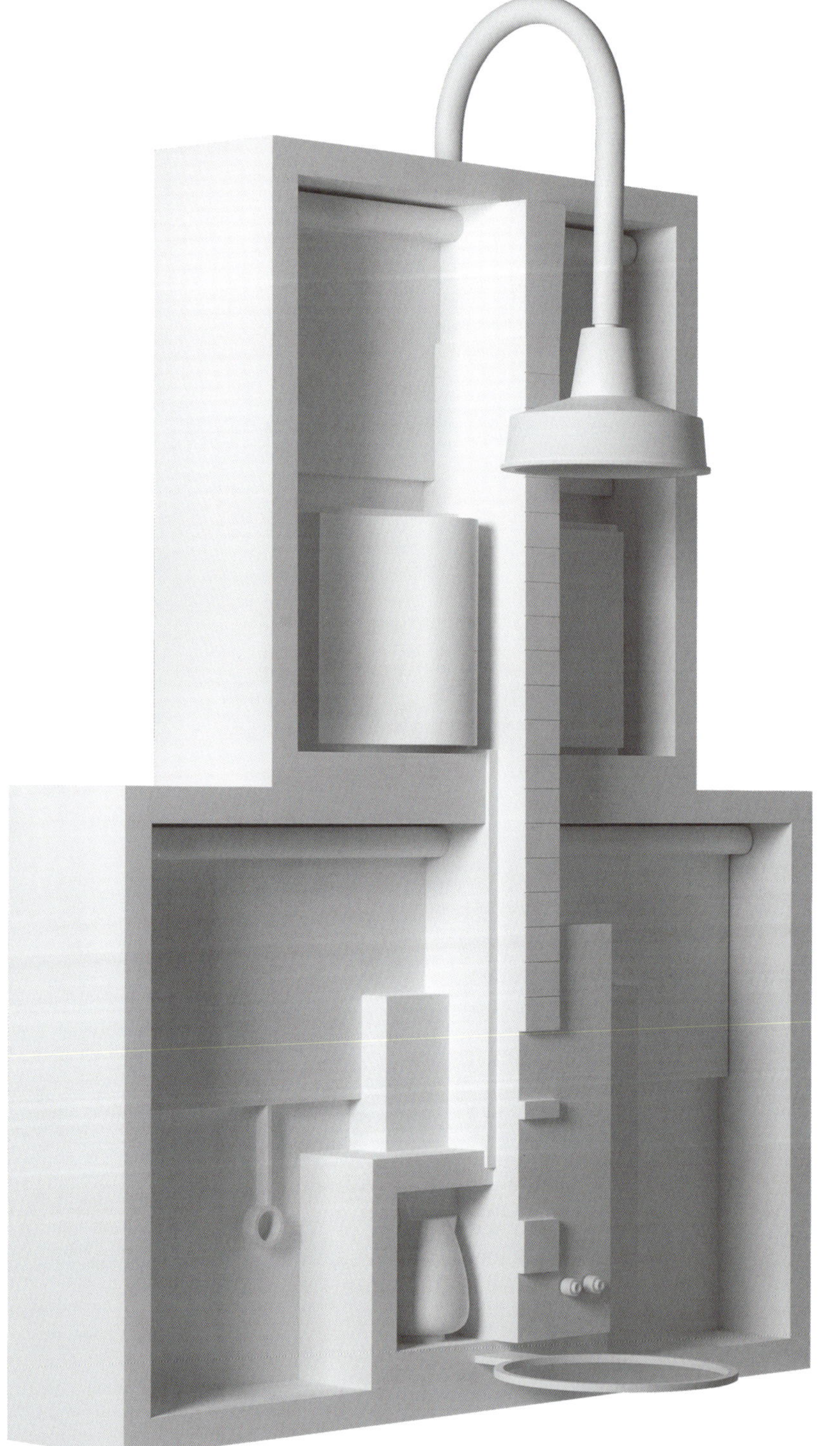

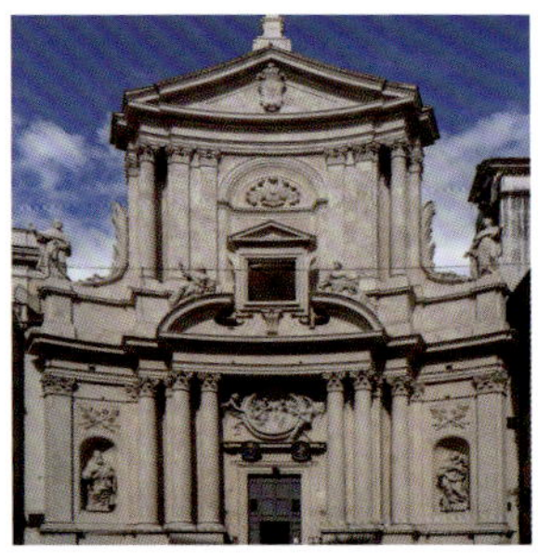

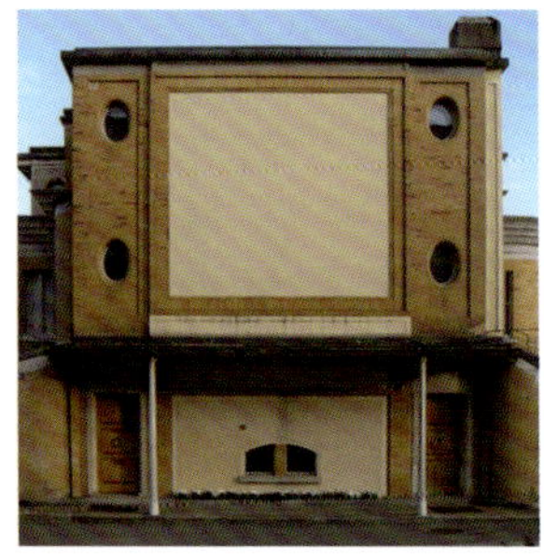

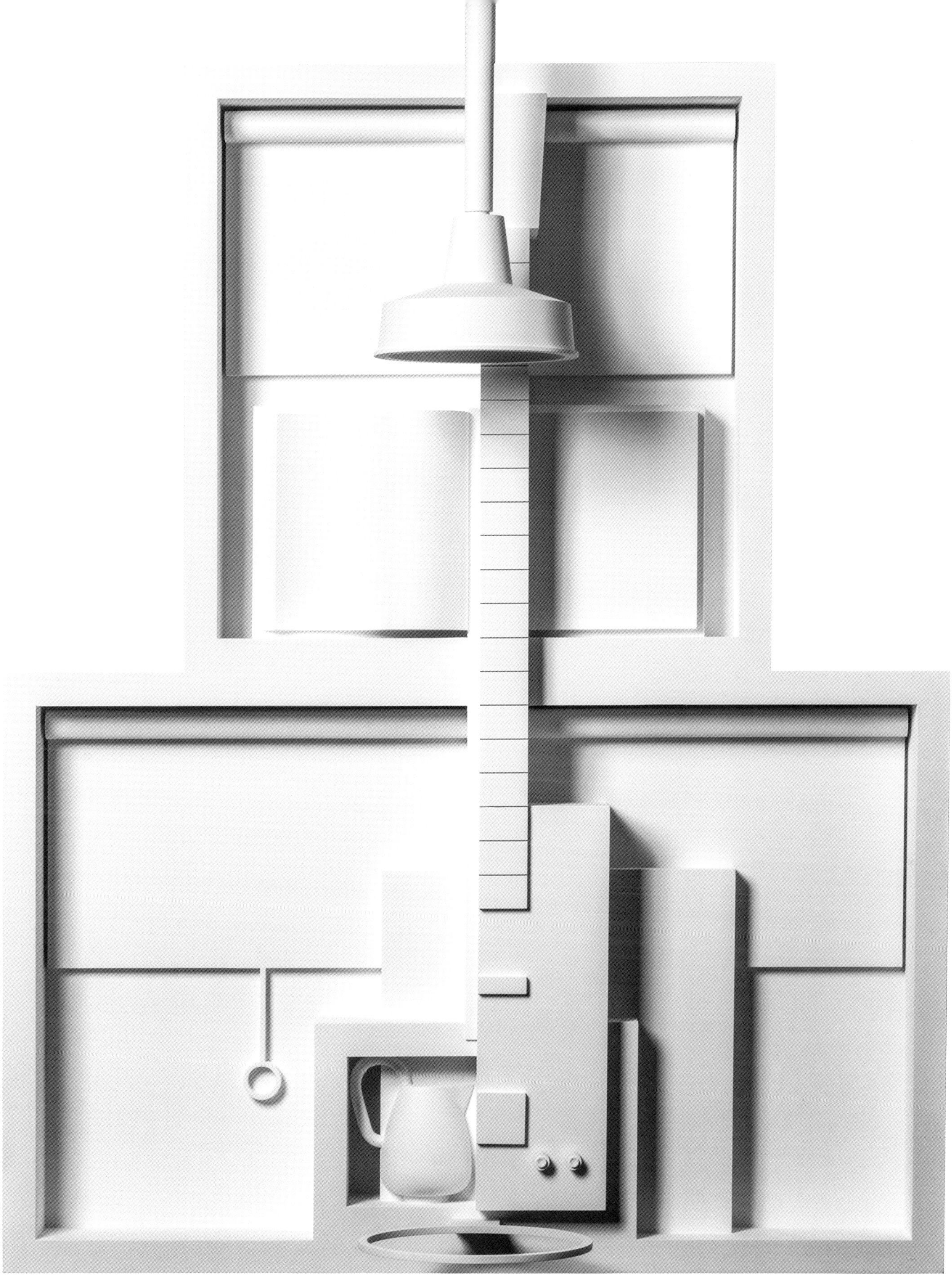

WHITE COMPOSITION 11

2024
ACRYLIC ON WOOD, PLYWOOD AND URETHANE
14.5 X 20 INCHES

This double square is an open book. The left page is curved and blank. The right page is flat and articulated. The 3D illustration is of a vessel. The image is framed by the reader's spectacles. The center of the composition is reinforced by a ribbon bookmark.

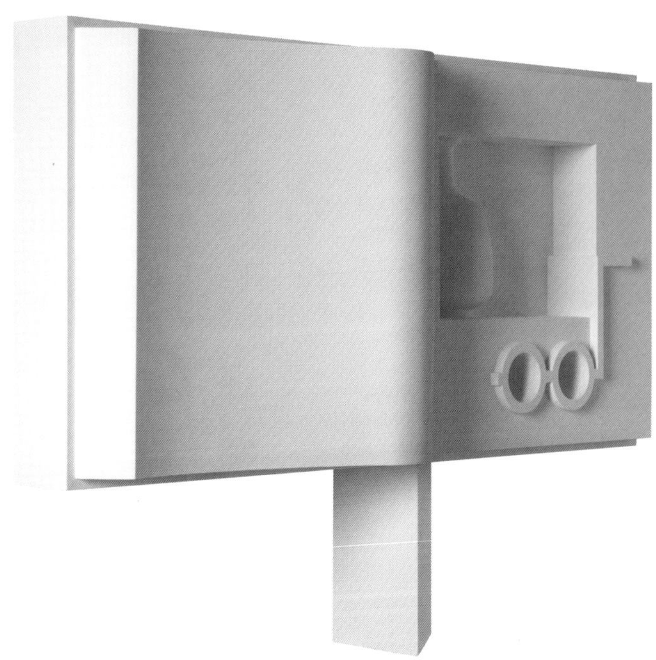

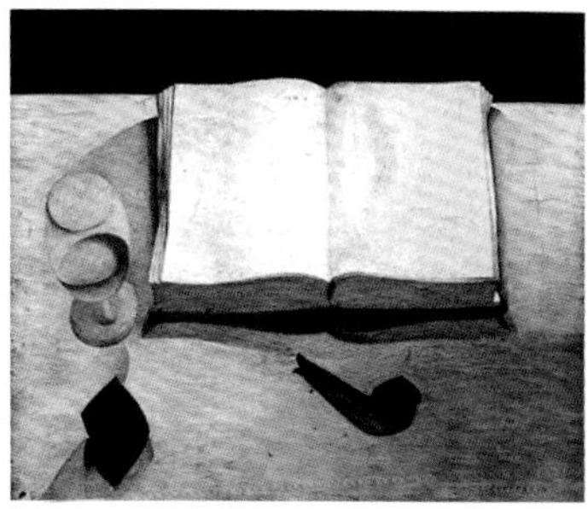

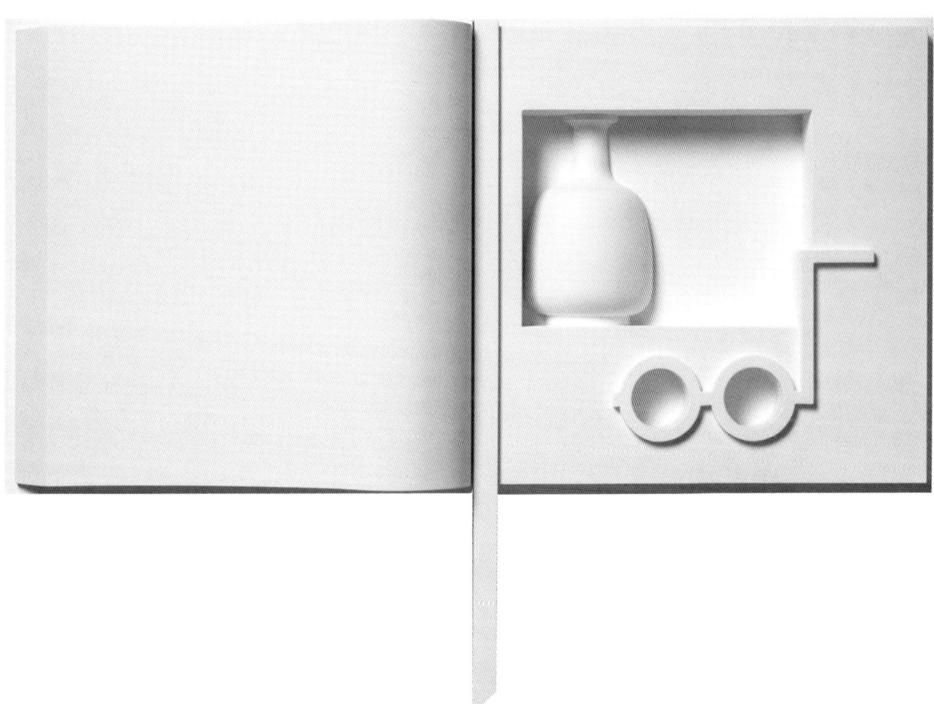

WHITE COMPOSITION 12

2024
ACRYLIC ON WOOD, PLYWOOD AND STEEL
96 X 48 INCHES

This installation along with other supportive material (see Appendix 1) was exhibited in a small room culminating the exhibition at a83 Gallery. It was originally intended to be just a simple shelf on which was placed random examples of some of the object types used in the *White Compositions.* However, it gradually evolved into a white wall composition occupying the entire wall surface. The vacancy of the composition was inspired by *La Cheminée* (1918), a painting by Charles Edouard Jeanneret that I always believed in (below).

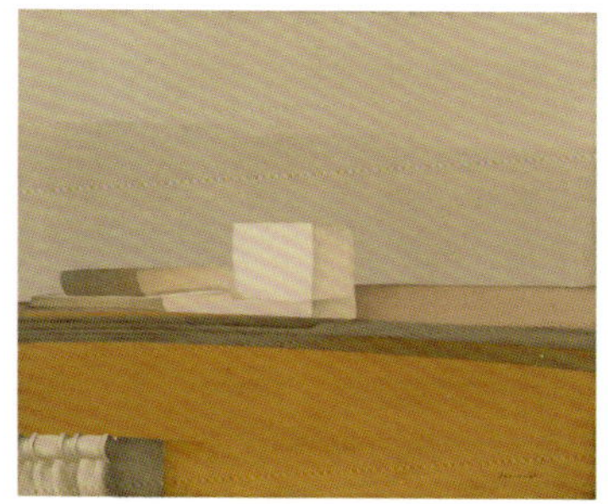

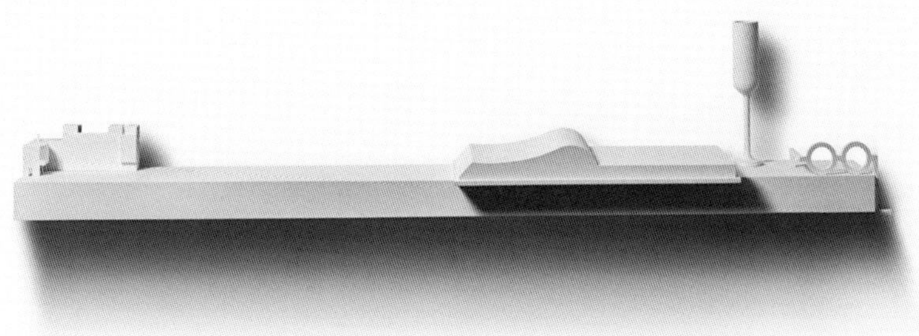

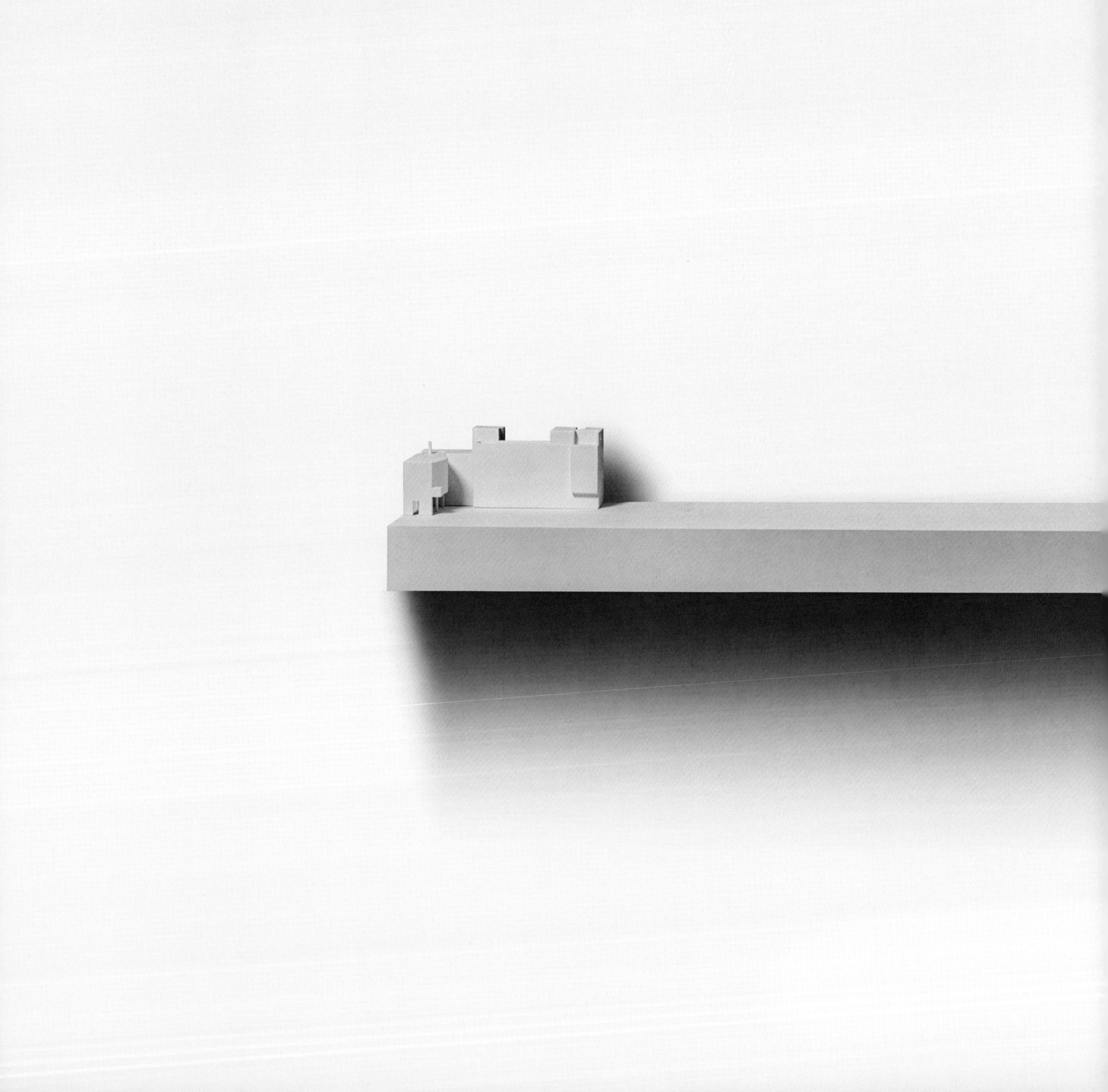

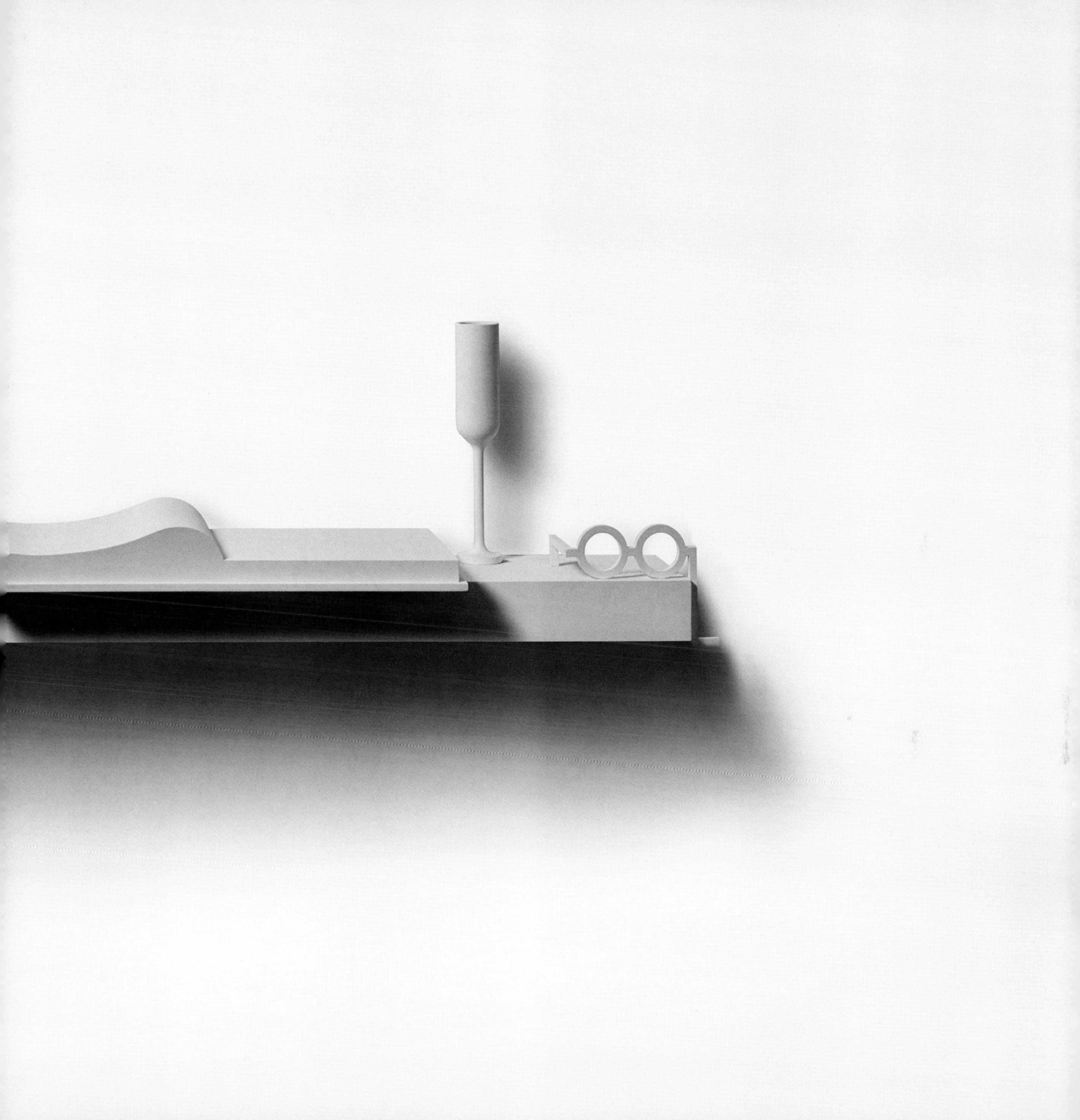

APPENDIX 1

Included here are images of the seven framed drawings included in the small room culminating the exhibition of the *White Compositions* at a83 Gallery.

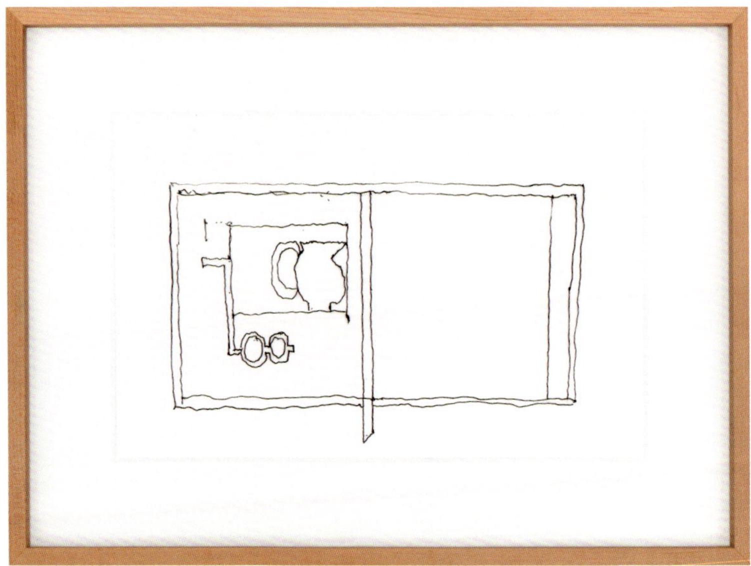

WHITE COMPOSITION 11 STUDY, 2024, INK ON VELLUM, 12 X 18 INCHES

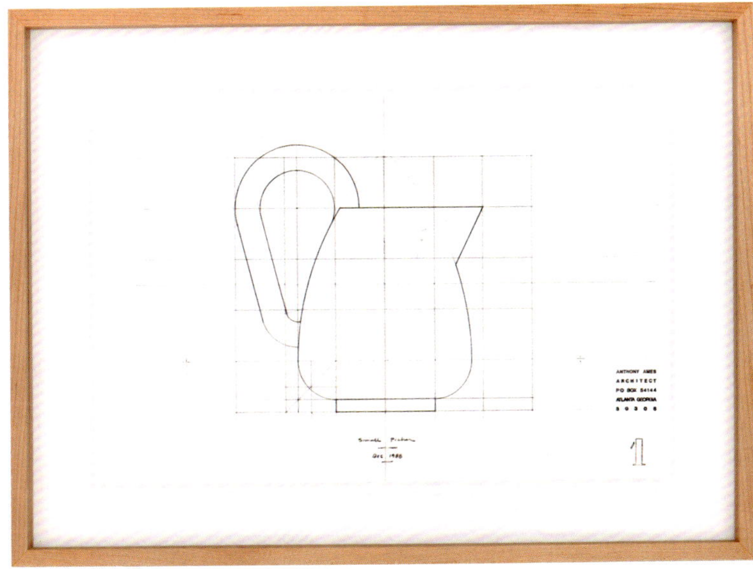

SMALL PITCHER, 1989, GRAPHITE ON VELLUM, 12 X 18 INCHES

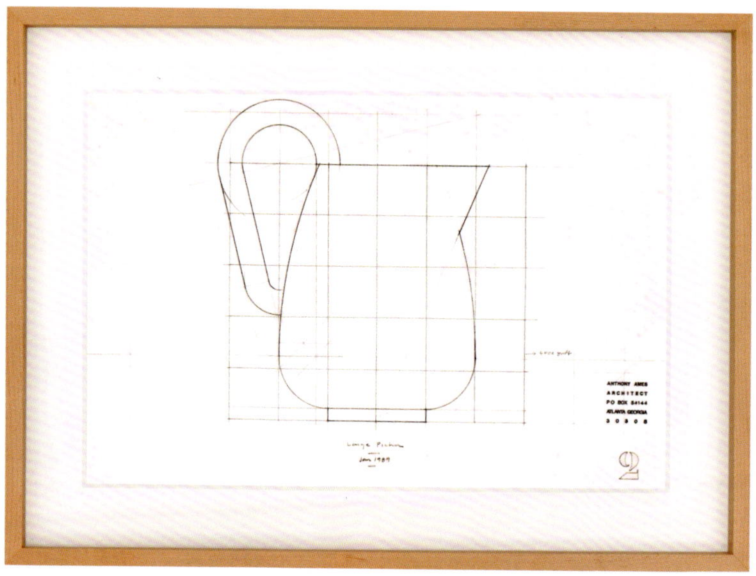

LARGE PITCHER, 1989, GRAPHITE ON VELLUM, 12 X 18 INCHES

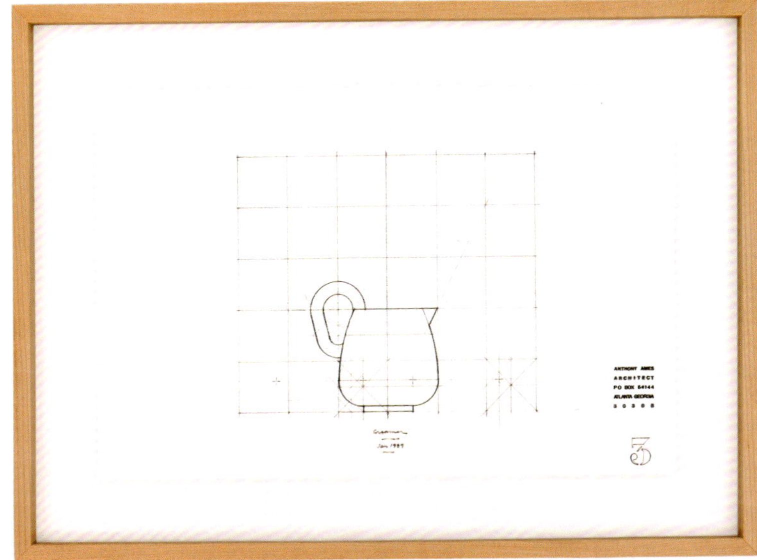

CREAMER, 1989, GRAPHITE ON VELLUM, 12 X 18 INCHES

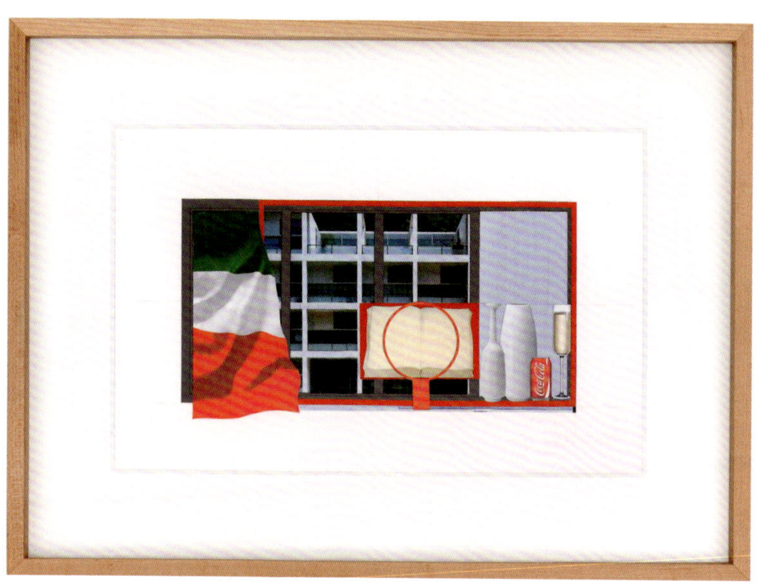

WHITE COMPOSITION 5 COLLAGE, 2012, MIXED MEDIA, 6 X 12 INCHES

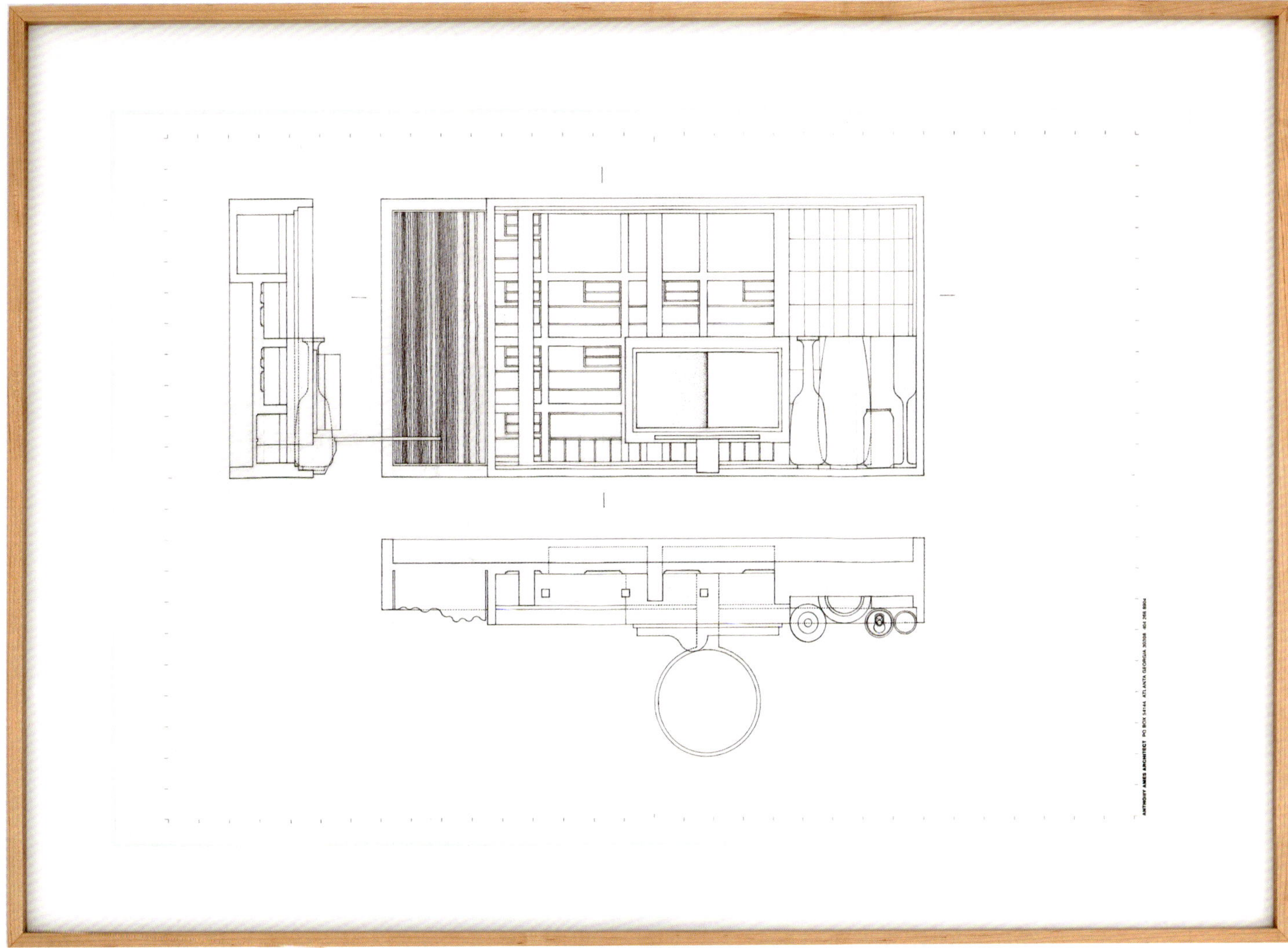

WHITE COMPOSION 5 STUDY, 2012, INK ON VELLUM, 24 X 36 INCHES

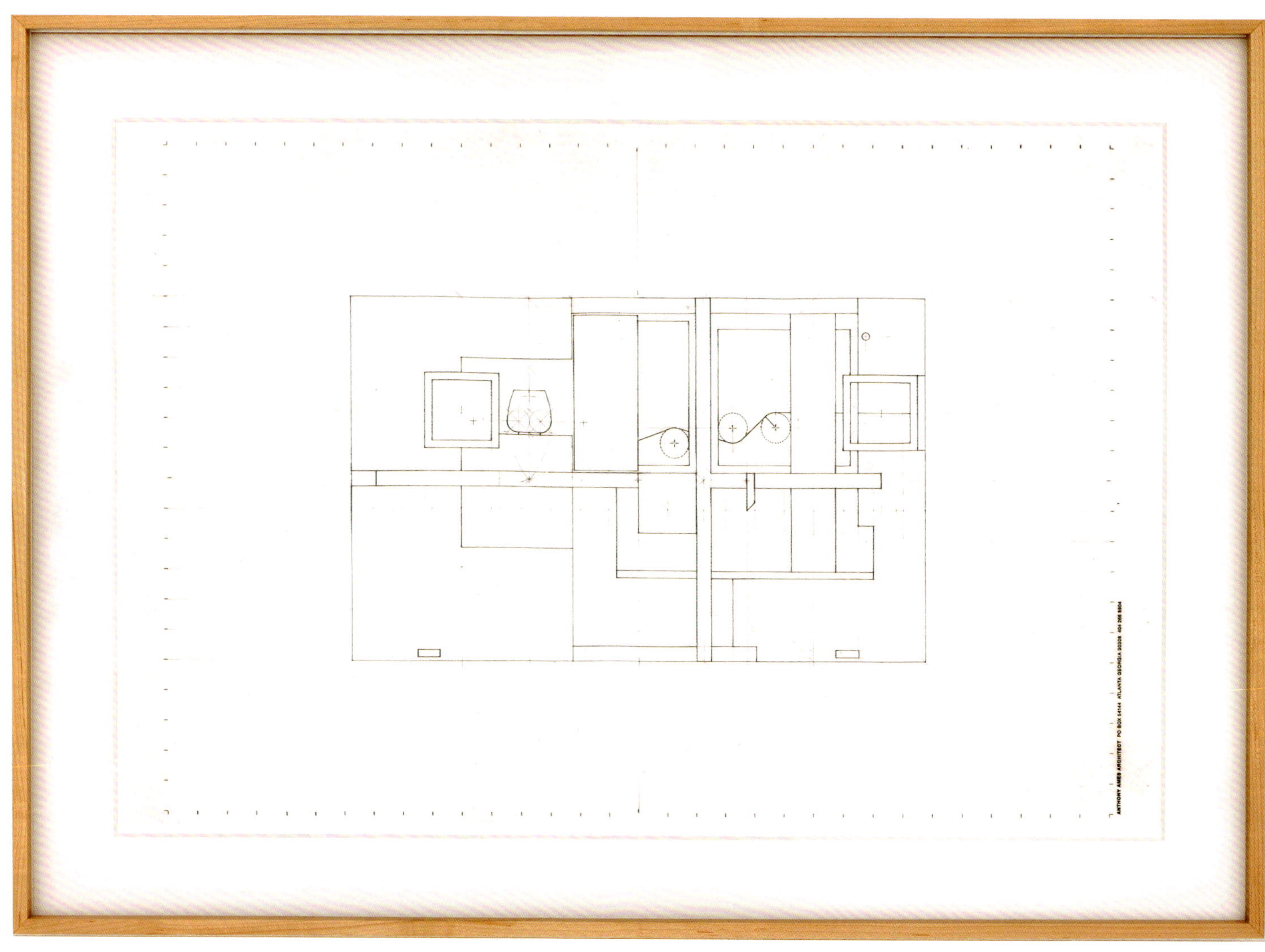

WHITE COMPOSITION 4 STUDY, 2011, GRAPHITE ON VELLUM, 24 X 36 INCHES

APPENDIX 2

Included here are images of a typical set of working drawings used to construct the *White Compositions* as referenced on pages 14 and 17.

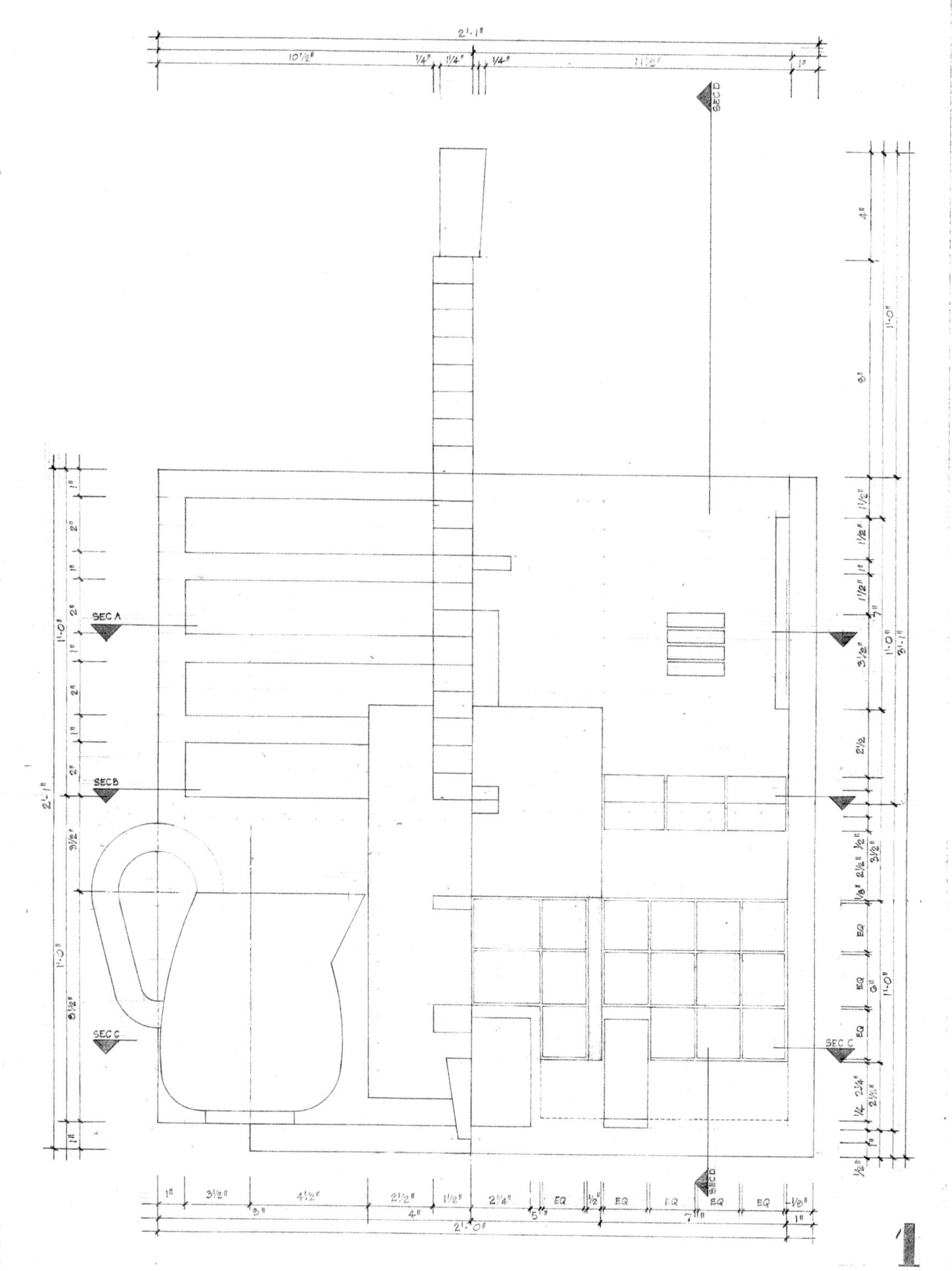
2'-1"
10½"
1/4"
1¼"
1/4"
11½"
1"
SEC D
SEC A
SEC B
SEC C
SEC C
1'-0"
2'-1"
3'-1"
1'-0"
1'-0"
1"
3½"
4½"
2½"
1½"
2¼"
EQ
EQ
EQ
EQ
EQ
3"
4"
5"
7"
2'-0"
1"
1

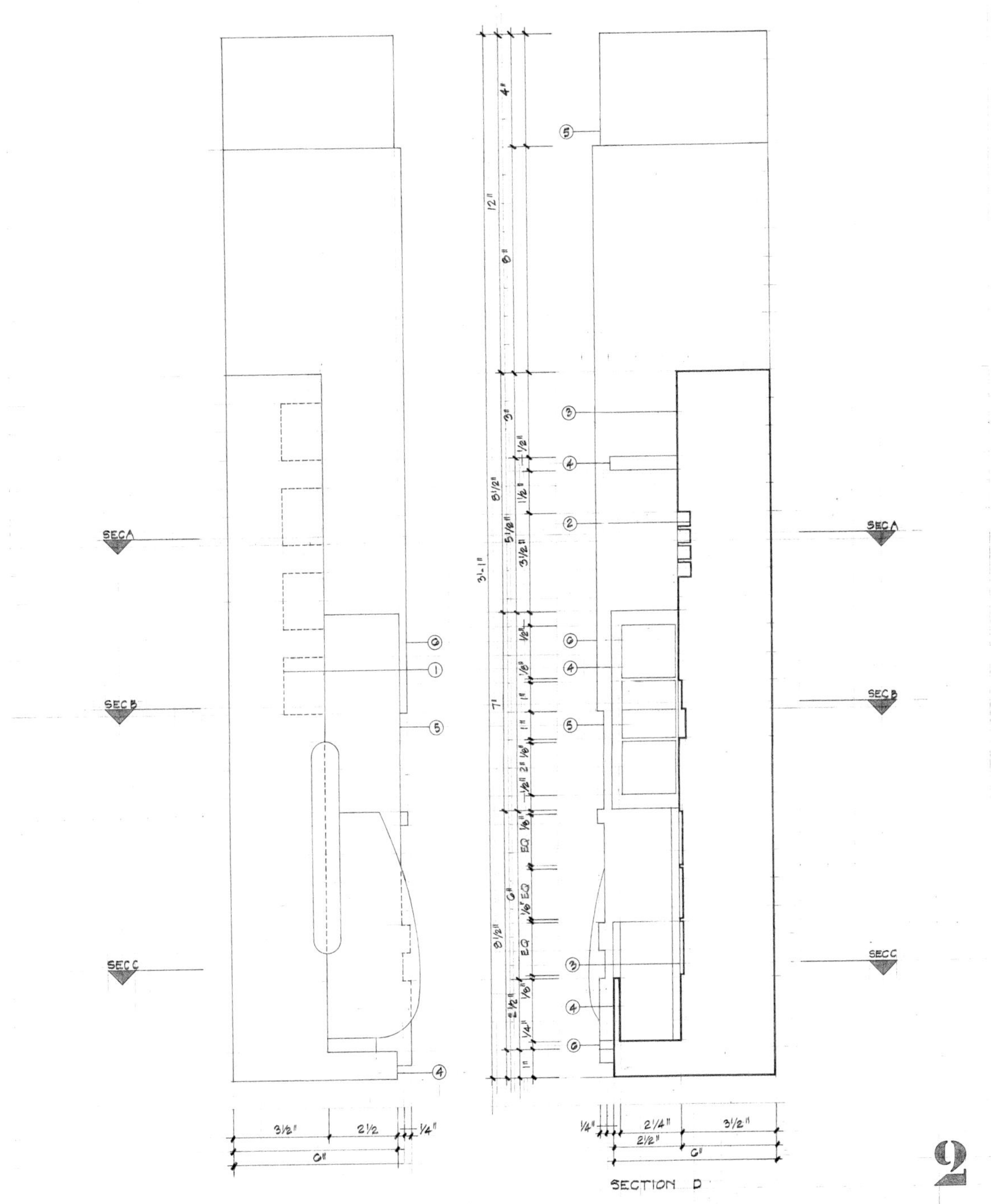
SEC A
SEC B
SEC C
SECTION D
3 1/2"
2 1/2
1/4"
6"
2 1/4"
3 1/2"
2 1/2"
4"
12"
8"
3"
7"
3'-1"
EQ
2

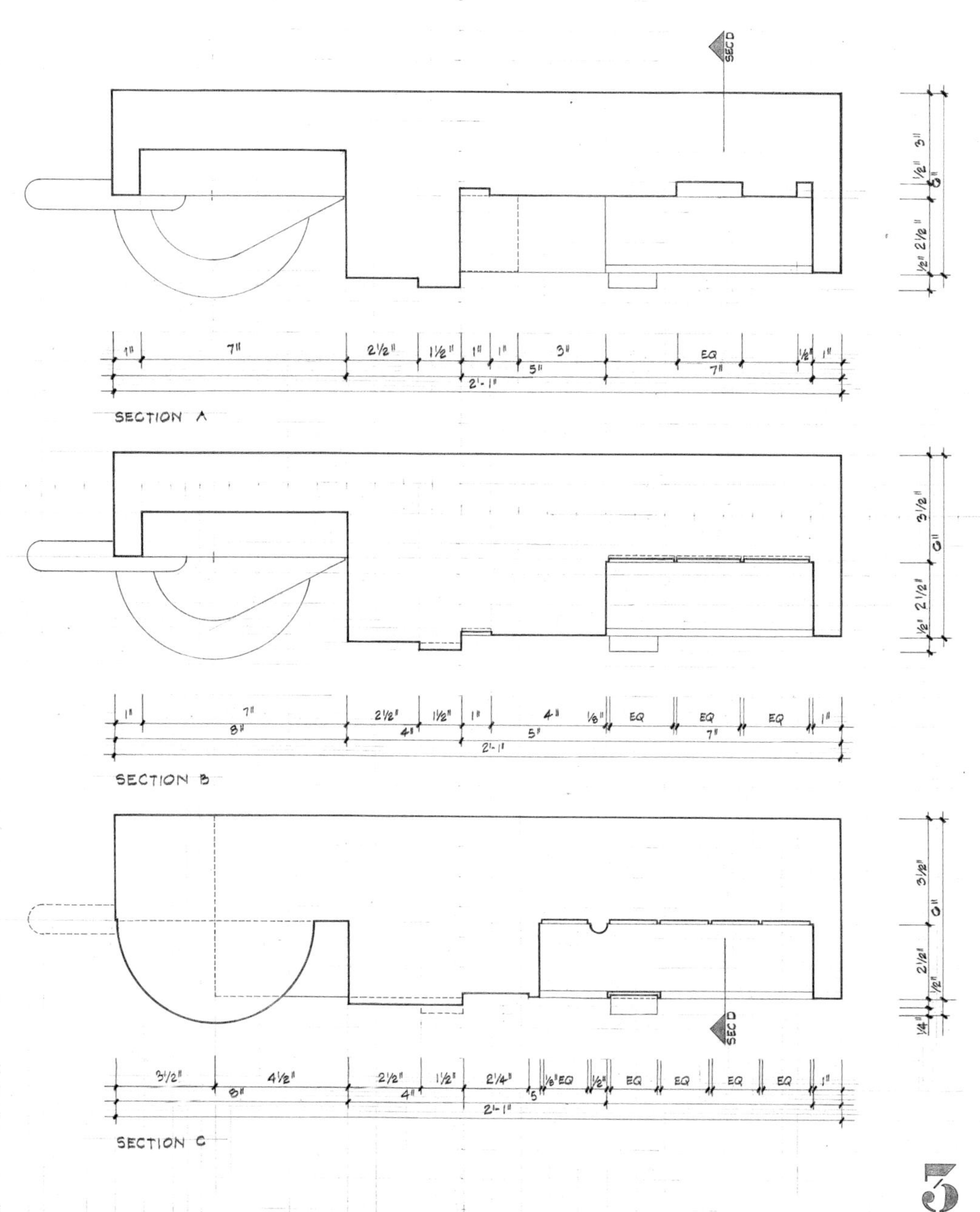
SEC D
SECTION A
SECTION B
SECTION C
2'-1"
3

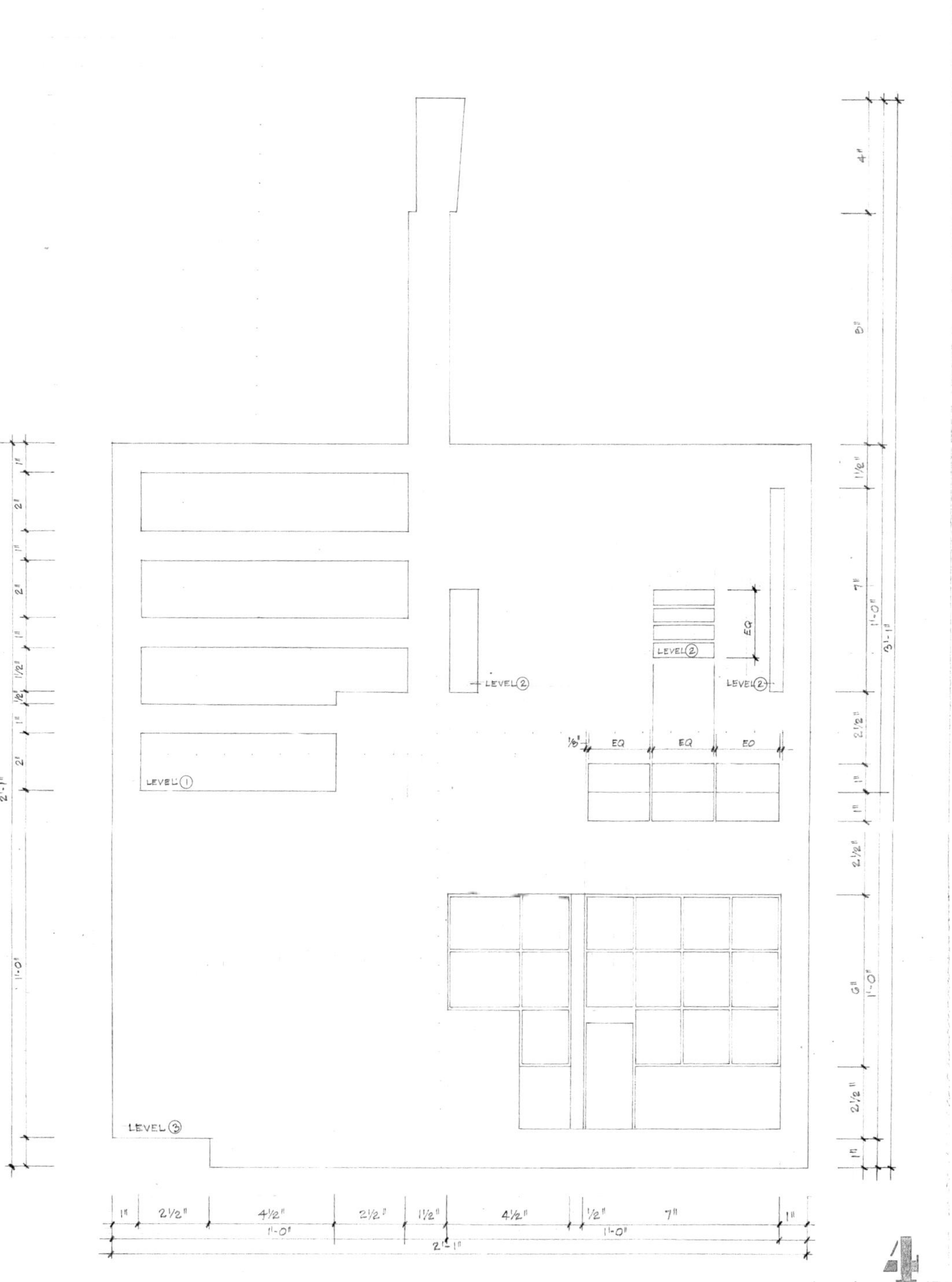

LEVEL 1
LEVEL 2
LEVEL 2
LEVEL 2
LEVEL 3
EQ
EQ
EQ
EQ
2'-1"
1'-0"
3'-1"
1'-0"
1'-0"
1'-0"
1" 2½" 4½" 2½" 1½" 4½" ½" 7" 1"
2'-1"
4

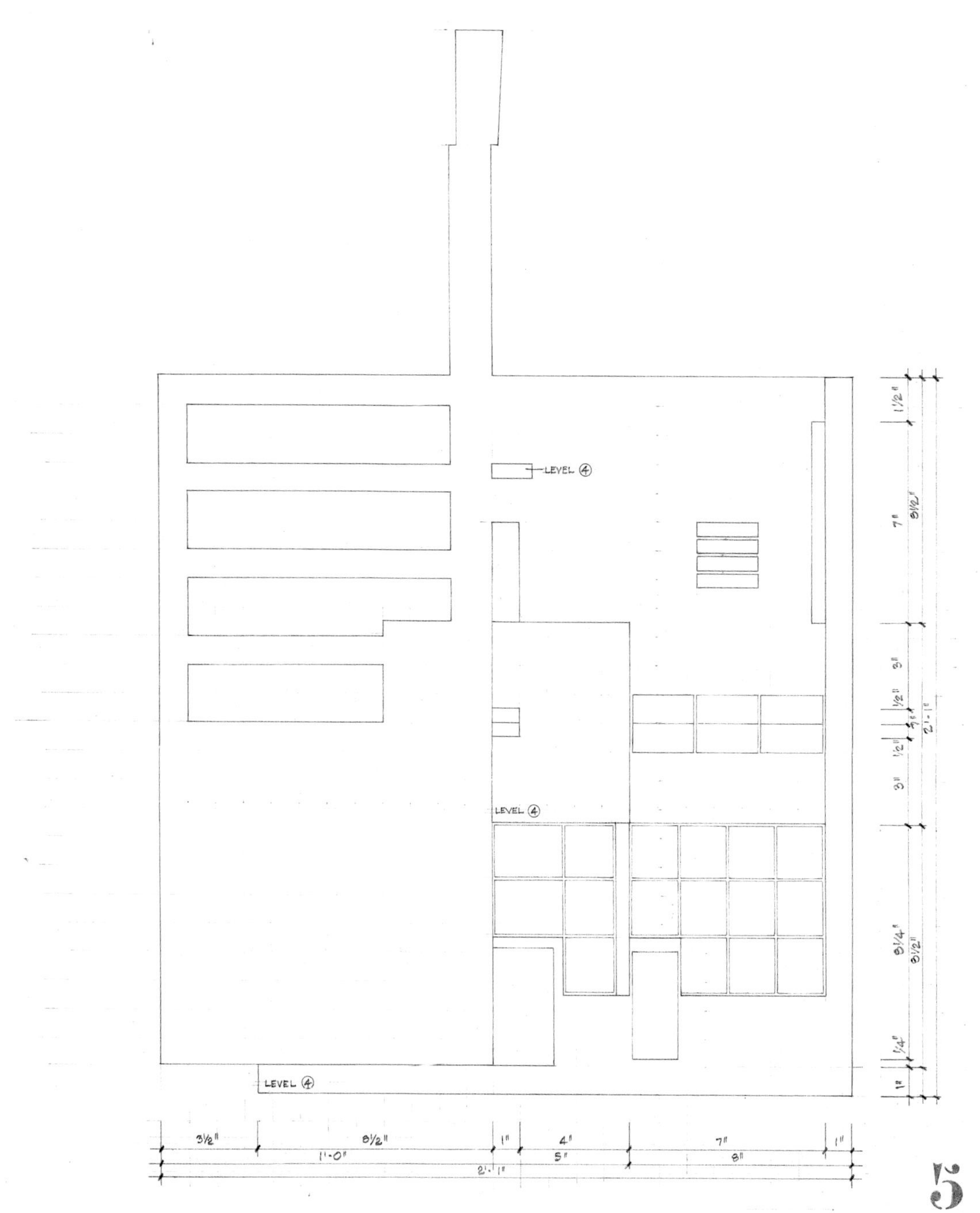
LEVEL 4
LEVEL 4
LEVEL 4
1½"
7"
8½"
3"
½"
1"
½"
3"
2'-1"
8¼"
8½"
¼"
1"
3½"
8½"
1"
4"
7"
1"
1'-0"
5"
8"
2'-1"
5

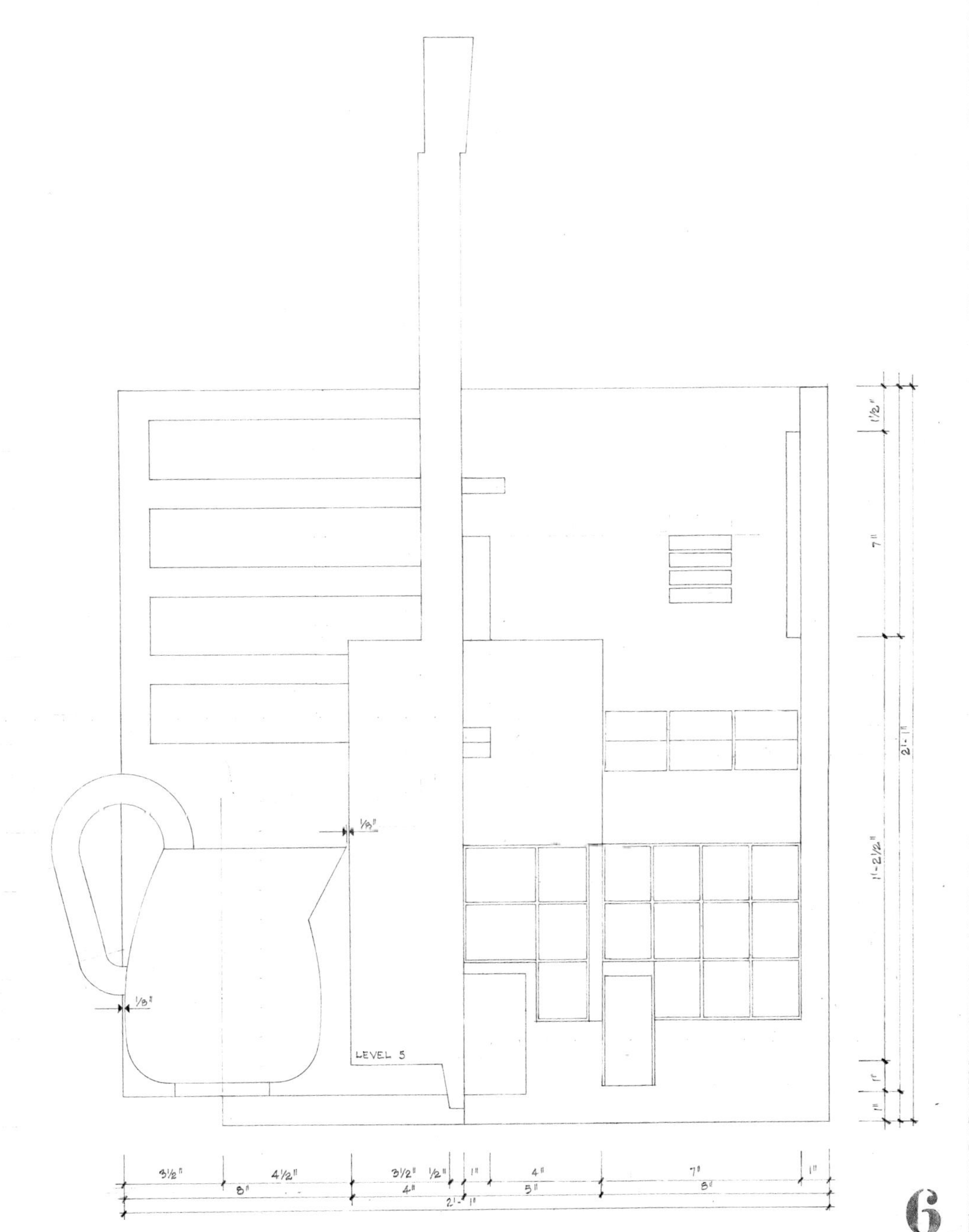
LEVEL 5
1/8"
1/8"
3½"
4½"
3½"
½"
1"
4"
7"
1"
8"
4"
5"
8"
2'-1"
1½"
7"
1'-2½"
2'-1"
1"
1"
6

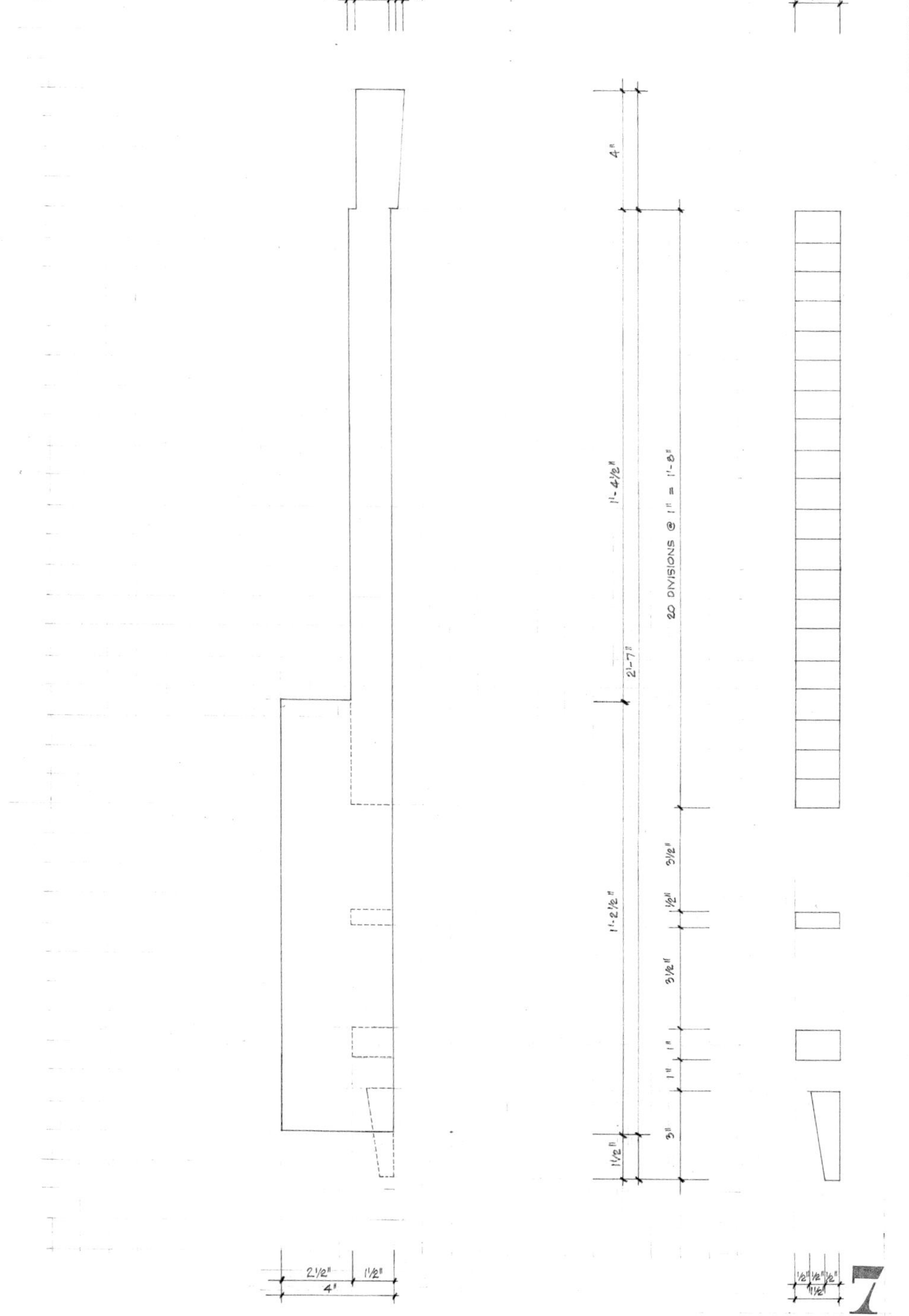
20 DIVISIONS @ 1" = 1'-8"
2'-7"
1'-4½"
1'-2½"
4"
2½"
1½"
4"
7

POSTSCRIPT

The lure of something mysterious is the feeling that something unknowable might be knowable. In the *White Compositions,* as much as they are a superimposition of architectural elements one can identify, they are also mixed with favorite objects and references from a personal life which are harder to pinpoint. Here there is something else at play. Their accessability relies on a known method of seeing architecture ... a code that promotes investigation into a private obsession that is didactic, intuitive and empirical, that is transferable and rewarding.

Daisy Ames

SELECTED EXHIBITIONS

White Compositions
a83 Gallery
New York, New York
May - July 2024

Fifty Paintings
a83 Gallery
New York, New York
July - September 2022

Object-Type Landscapes
Casa Curutchet
La Plata, Argentina
September 2015

Common Ground
13th International Architecture Exhibition
La Biennale di Venezia
Venice, Italy
August - November 2012

Type-Scapes
Cornell University
Milstein Hall Gallery
College of Architecture, Art and Planning
Ithaca, New York
March 2012

Architects as Artists
Swan Coach House Gallery
Atlanta History Center
Atlanta, Georgia
January - February 2012

Object-Type Landscapes
University of Maryland
Kibel Gallery
School of Architecture, Planning and Preservation
College Park, Maryland
Fall 2011

Residential Landscapes
High Museum of Art
Atlanta, Georgia
April - September 2009

Architecture of Anthony Ames
Syracuse University
School of Architecture
Syracuse, New York
Winter 2002

Object-Type Landscapes
Kansas State University
College of Architecture
Manhattan, Kansas
Winter 1998

Object-Type Landscapes
University of Tennessee
Ewing Gallery
School of Architecture and Planning
Knoxville, Tennessee
Fall 1996

Object-Type Landscapes
Syracuse University
School of Architecture
Syracuse, New York
Spring 1996

Object-Type Landscapes
Farrington Gallery
Atlanta, Georgia
Spring 1994

Anthony Ames
Current Work
University of Maryland
School of Architecture
College Park, Maryland
Fall 1990

Anthony Ames / Drawings
University of Alabama
Moody Gallery of Art
Tuscaloosa, Alabama
Summer 1989

Anthony Ames / Drawings
University of Arkansas
School of Architecture
Fayetteville, Arkansas
Spring 1989

Anthony Ames / Drawings
University of Virginia
School of Architecture
Charlottesville, Virginia
Spring 1989

The Experimental Tradition:
25 Years of American
Architectural Competitions
1960 - 1985
The Academy of Design
New York, New York
Summer 1989

Anthony Ames / Drawings
University of Texas
School of Architecture and
Environmental Design
Arlington, Texas
September 1988

The Emerging Generation in U.S.A.
GA Gallery
Tokyo, Japan
Fall 1987

Three Firms
Columbia University
School of Architecture and Urban Planning
New York, New York
Spring 1986

Architects for Social Responsibility
Max Protetch Gallery
New York, New York
Spring 1985

Freidrichstadt
Rhode Island School of Design
Providence, Rhode Island
Spring 1985

Ten Drawings
Ballenford Architectural Books Gallery
Toronto, Ontario
Winter 1985

Annual Exhibition
American Academy in Rome
Rome, Italy
Spring 1984

Ten Drawings
University of Virginia
School of Architecture
Charlottesville, Virginia
Spring 1983

Ten Drawings
Harvard Graduate School of Design
Cambridge, Massachusetts
Winter 1982

Ten Drawings
KIPNIS: Works of Art
Atlanta, Georgia
Winter 1982

Archifest Group Exhibition
Peachtree Center
Atlanta, Georgia
October 1982

Drawings by Architects
KIPNIS: Works of Art
Atlanta, Georgia
January 1982

Archifest Group Exhibition
Peachtree Center
Atlanta, Georgia
October 1981

Four + 2
Nexus Gallery
Atlanta, Georgia
Fall 1980

IMAGE CREDITS:

p. 5 Chuck Pittman
pp. 8,9 Olympia Shannon
p. 12 Olympia Shannon
p. 16 Olympia Shannon
p. 17 Alan Balfour (L & C)
p. 17 Jornod et Jornod, *Le Corbusier, Catalogue raisonné de l'oeuvre peint, Tome I* (Milan, Skira, 2005) p. 331 (R)
p. 18 Jornod et Jornod, *Le Corbusier, Catalogue raisonné de l'oeuvre peint, Tome I* (Milan, Skira, 2005) p. 349 (L)
p. 18 Josep Palau i Fabre, *Picasso Cubisme 1907 - 1917* (New York, Rizzoli, 1990) p. 324 (R)
p. 19 Swid Powell (L), Kynaston & McShine, *Joseph Cornell* (New York, Museum of Modern Art, 1980) plate xxii (R)
p. 20 Chuck Pittman (L & R)
p. 21 AAA
p. 22 Olympia Shannon
p. 23 Chuck Pittman (L, C & R)
p. 24 AAA (L & R)
p. 25 AAA (L, C & R)
p. 26 Olympia Shannon
p. 27 Chuck Pittman
p. 28 Chuck Pittman
p. 34 Chuck Pittman
p. 37 Richard Pare, *Le Corbusier, The Buildings* (London, Thames & Hudson, 2018) p. 185
p. 41 AAA
p. 44 Dobney and Inciardi, *Play It Loud* (New York, Metropolitan Museum of Art, 2019) p. 43
p. 46 AAA
p. 48 *Oeuvre Complete Vol. 1* (p. 159)
p. 51 Jornod et Jornod, *Le Corbusier, Catalogue raisonné de l'oeuvre peint, Tome I* (Milan, Skira, 2005) p. 349
p. 54 Columnsss (L), Utopia/Dystopia (R)
p. 56 Jornod et Jornod, *Le Corbusier, Catalogue raisonné de l'oeuvre peint, Tome I* (Milan, Skira, 2005) p. 331
p. 58 Jornod et Jornod, *Le Corbusier, Catalogue raisonné de l'oeuvre peint, Tome I* (Milan, Skira, 2005) p. 328

All *White Compositions* photographed by Chuck Pittman.

ACKNOWLEDGEMENTS

I would like to thank my faithful assistant for forty years, Clark Tefft. This book would not have been possible without his assistance nor would the previous books or the work in the office. A special thank you goes to Norbert Schaum, Kyle Marchisen and Tripp Edwards, the master craftsmen who constructed the compositions. I would like to thank Chuck Pittman for his exceptional individual photographs of the *White Compositions* and Olympia Shannon for her beautiful photographs of the *White Compositions* installation at the a83 Gallery. Next I would like to thank those who contributed essays to the book. Clara Syme with her partner Owen Nichols currated two exhibitions of the work at Gallery a83 - formerly The John Nichols Gallery. Their advocacy has been primary in allowing me to exhibit the paintings and compositions. Clara's introduction intelligently provides guidance, insight and credibility. She is genuine, sincere and candid, three things I could never be. Thank you to Alan Balfour for lending his knowledge of the game of architecture and his willingness to participate in that game. He provides an historically informative narrative - real or imagined - and discovers or invents a contextual universe that gives the work validity. Thank you to Courtney Coffman for applying her unique writing skills and articulation to inventing an original scenario contributing to the discussion of the work. I appreciate her audacity, ambition and modesty. And finally I would like to thank Peter Eisenman for his generosity with his ideas, his knowledge and his thoughts, but most of all for his time which he used to make the discipline of architecture a more meaningful, provocative and stimulating place to spend a life. And thank you Cynthia Davidson. Lastly, thank you Daisy Ames who wrote the postscript and is the youngest of the ducklings. In conclusion, I would like to thank Gordon Goff and his assistant Jake Anderson for their expertise in book production.

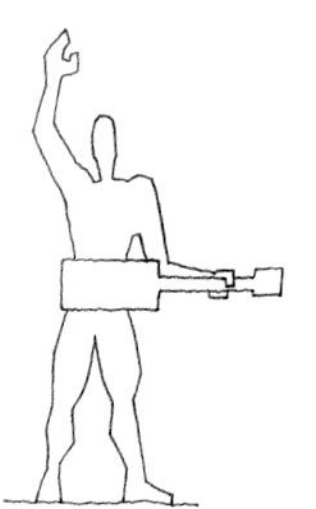